Ploughboy'

The Life of Sir Ge

BY NOEL G. EDWARDS

Foreword by

Bert Hazell, CBE
Former President of the
National Union of Agricultural and Allied Workers

EDITED WITH AN INTRODUCTION BY ALUN HOWKINS,
Professor of Social History, University of Sussex

Centre of East Anglian Studies
University of East Anglia

1998

ISBN 0 906219 46 9

Printed by Postprint, Taverner House, East Harling, Norfolk.

Contents

Foreword

By Bert Hazell, CBE, JP,

Member of Parliament for North Norfolk, 1964-1970 and President of the National Union of Agricultural & Allied Workers, 1966-1978.

As a young Norfolk farm worker, I joined the then National Union of Agricultural Workers upon leaving school in 1921. To me, as to so many farm workers, the name of George Edwards was a living reality, for he was the leader we knew so well, who spoke at our rallies, and who encouraged us during the great Norfolk Farm Workers Strike of 1923, in which I participated.

It is fitting that his adopted son should place on record the life and work of one who created and led for so many years a Trade Union for Farm Workers, a task which had been attempted in earlier years, but with only a modicum of success for various reasons. Today, ninety years after the initial meeting in North Walsham, the NUAW (as a section of the TGWU) is still a very lively and active organisation throughout England and Wales, with a small foothold in Scotland. Many of the objectives of our pioneer founder and his colleagues have been achieved, though obviously in the changed circumstances of the present age there is a continuing vital role for the Union to play, both at home and abroad, and particularly within the context of the European Community.

George Edwards, like so many of our earlier Trade Union pioneers, derived much of his strength, enthusiasm in the cause of justice, and fair treatment from his close ties with the Methodist Church and his deep religious convictions. We would do well if in our time we would look back to the source from which so many of the early Trade Union leaders derived their inspiration.

I was privileged to know George Edwards personally, joined the crowds at the Wymondham meeting after his success in the 1923 election, and, many years later, followed his path to the Houses of Parliament and as President of the Union he created. I served with him on the Executive Committee of the South Norfolk Divisional Labour Party for a number of years.

I commend this story to you. It is a reminder of the grim times our forbears experienced, and the value of having an active rural Trade Union to raise the status of those who produce our food.

Introduction

George Edwards's Autobiography, *From Crow Scaring to Westminster*, and its 1957 reprint, has long been out of print and difficult to obtain. In his latter days he received many requests for its up-date. The task was beyond him. He expressed the wish that I might at some future date be able to attempt it. This I did, but unfortunately due to my own family financial position and the continuing economic depression over the years, its publication has not been possible, despite the support of a few prominent folk. But now due to the very kind help and effort of Alun Howkins and the support of the Centre of East Anglian Studies at the University of East Anglia publication has been possible.

This book does not pretend to be a social history, but the account of a very humble person who, born in poverty, despite deprivation, physical suffering and the sacrifices made, rose above that through great courage and deep religious faith. He saw he had a mission to endeavour to raise the standard of life, socially, morally and spiritually of his fellows and lived to see some progress made in that.

My thanks are due to Alun Howkins, my old friend Bert Hazell for his foreword and to all who over the years assisted with my script and provided data for it. Amongst which are: the National Union of Agricultural and Allied Workers, the Clerks (before Local Government reorganisation) of Walsingham RDC and Fakenham Town Council. I should also like to thank Linda Merricks for reading the manuscript, Richard Wilson, Director of the Centre of East Anglian Studies at UEA Norwich for his editorial assistance and Emma Hazell and Mavis Wesley, both of the Centre, for setting up the book on their word processors.

Noel G. Edwards.
Fakenham, Norfolk, 1997

Editor's Introduction

Alun Howkins

Ninety-two years ago this year, in the clubroom of the Angel Hotel at North Walsham in Norfolk, what is now the Agricultural Trades Section of the Transport and General Workers Union was founded as the Eastern Counties Agricultural Labourers and Small Holders Union. The central figure at that meeting was a fifty-six year old farm worker and brick maker from near Aylsham called George Edwards. He was already a veteran of the labour movement. He began his career as an 'agitator' (a noble word, not an insult, for his generation!) at a meeting in Alby in June 1872 where he spoke at a meeting to found a branch of Joseph Arch's National Agricultural Labourers Union in the village.[1] He died, still in harness, sixty years later, in Fakenham.

The story which follows is the life of this remarkable man, and in that respect parts of it are unique to him. Yet in others the life of George Edwards, 'Our George' to two generations of Norfolk farm workers, could stand for the lives of those men and women. Born into terrible poverty at the end of the 'hungry forties' of the last century, he began work scaring crows aged six in 1856. These were years of great agricultural prosperity - of what was called 'high farming'. A growing industrial and urban population, and little foreign competition, ensured that wheat prices remained high from the 1840s until the end of the 1870s. In Norfolk the farmers used to say looking back to that period, 'they brought gold and left it at your barn door'.

Little of this prosperity reached the farm worker. Edwards started work on a boy's wage of a shilling a week for six days. Normal enough when adult wages were little more than eight shillings for the same hours. During the 'golden age' of high farming money wages increased, perhaps by as much as a third. By 1872, when the first farm workers unions were formed the Norfolk labourer could take home twelve or thirteen shillings a week, but the reality was that well over half that increase had been eaten away by higher prices.[2]

The rural poor responded to this in different ways. George's father, like many, was forced to steal food from the fields and was sent to prison for it. Thousands poached, mostly rabbits and hares, and frequently suffered a similar fate. A few, driven by hunger to anger and then to hatred, burnt ricks or even maimed animals. Others began to look to their own collective strength. The first signs of this change can be detected in the 1830s when Robert Key, a Yarmouth coal heaver began to preach a gospel of 'full and free salvation' in the villages and to recruit those brought into the fold into

Primitive Methodism. This was the faith that George Edwards was to join in 1869 and which, like his radicalism, was to stay with him throughout his life.

Primitive Methodism had begun in 1811 in Tunstall in Staffordshire as a plebeian offshoot of the Wesleyan Methodists. From the start it was marked by a fierce independence of mind and a distrust of the mighty and great. It spread through the English Midlands and reached Norfolk in the 1820s when Robert Key was converted. To those who became members it gave great spiritual and personal strength. On the basis of this they built their chapels and created the culture that came from them. This culture encouraged self-help and self education. Many, like George, learned to read and write under the chapel's walls, ultimately becoming lay preachers, who were always the majority of those who led the scattered flock. Yet even very late in life George, in his writing, continued to use Norfolk dialect. See for example his letter to the Lord Chancellor in Chapter 9.

Perhaps more important it taught organisation - how to speak in public, how to run a meeting, how to organise a congregation - all of which they transferred later to trades unions and radical politics. Finally, it gave these men (and some women) a dignity and belief in their own worth as the humblest of Christ's band on earth which pushed them to confront evil in all its forms - from un-Godliness, to drink, and ultimately to social injustice. It was these feelings and convictions that led so many Primitive Methodists into becoming activists in the Unions when they appeared after 1872. As the *Eastern Weekly Press* wrote, 'nearly all the leaders of the movement (are) God-fearing-men, and many of them had for twenty or thirty years past travelled hundreds of miles on the Sabbath, after having worked hard for six days, to preach the Gospel.'[3]

From its first meetings in Norfolk in the early Spring of 1872 the farm workers union movement grew rapidly. At first local unions sprung up, often in individual villages, but as the summer of that year turned to autumn they began to amalgamate, mostly into the National Agricultural Labourers Union (the one led by Joseph Arch) although some joined the Lincolnshire Labour League. As elsewhere in England the first two years of the union's existence was marked by success and euphoria. There were many local strikes in Norfolk and most saw wages raised. The union leaders, schooled in chapel, compared their movement to the freeing of Israel from the bondage of Egypt. However, the situation was soon to change when, in the spring of 1874, farmers in Suffolk and Cambridgeshire locked-out all union members. For five months the trade unions hung on, but in August they were forced to withdraw strike pay as their funds were all but gone. The locked out men, or some of them, went back to work and left the unions. Although the lock-out barely touched Norfolk, its shock waves did. In the autumn and winter of

1874-5 the euphoria vanished in the face of the chill wind from the south, and the labourers of Norfolk, as elsewhere, realised just how vulnerable they were.

Between 1874 and their final demise in 1896, the fortunes of the Norfolk unions fluctuated. Although the membership rose and fell, real gains were made as when the farm worker got the vote in 1884 and turned Norfolk to the Liberals in 1885. In 1889 the new County Council had working class representation on it, even if at this stage it was only one man, George Rix. For all this the union deserved a lot of credit. In the late 1870s some areas of Norfolk, 'duin' different,' split away from the National Union and formed what was to become the Norfolk and Norwich Amalgamated Labourers Union, a general union which sought to unionise not only farm workers, but also town labourers and working women in the county and its towns. It was here that George got his first taste of organising. At first, as in 1872, the Norfolk and Norwich union met with some success. However, a series of bitter conflicts, especially with the newly formed Farmers Federation in 1892-4, weakened the resolve of the members and, in 1896, the Union collapsed.

George Edwards, as the biography tells, was bitter and felt that his life's work was finished. However, he continued, as did others elsewhere in the county and in England, to work in the new county councils as well as in their smaller brethren in the parishes and districts. This work was to prove invaluable when in 1906 the 'call' came again to reform the union. This was a very different situation, and in consequence a very different union. Although chapel men still played a large part there was none of the almost religious fervour of 1872, rather there was a slow but steady growth, first in Norfolk, then elsewhere. Gains came, but like the growth of the union, they were gradual, a few pence here, a few hours there, but by the outbreak of the Great War in 1914 the condition of the farm worker had improved.

In 1913 George Edwards handed over his full time union work to 'younger men' especially Robert Walker, 'the General', as he became known in Norfolk. Through the war improvements continued as the nation and the farmers were forced by labour shortage and increased demand for home grown food to grant wage increases and better conditions. These reached their high point with the establishment of the first Wages Boards in 1917 which gave the Norfolk labourer 30 shillings a week and continued to raise wages until the summer of 1921 when they reached 45 shillings. Throughout the war union membership grew as did the farm workers' confidence. In 1918 the union for the first time officially supported Labour Party candidates in the General Election, and the following year saw a number of Labour gains in rural areas in local elections. The real triumph, however, came in 1920 when George was elected to Westminster from South Norfolk in a by-election. Although he lost his seat in the General Election in 1922 it was triumph for him and for the organised farm workers.

In 1921 the government, fiercely retrenching in the teeth of recession, removed support from agriculture and abolished the Wages Boards in what came to be known as the 'Great Betrayal.' Wages rapidly fell. By the spring of 1923 they were back to 25 shillings and the farmers sought a further reduction to 22s 6d. This was too much and the Norfolk strike began. Although he was sixty-three years old George Edwards took an active part in the strike, as Chapter 8 of this book shows. The strike lasted from 17 March until 23 April and ended in a negotiated settlement. Who 'won' was then, and is now, a matter of disagreement, but probably the most important thing is that the union survived, the wage cuts were stopped, and the workers of Norfolk left 'bloody but unbowed'.

The 1923 strike was the end of the 'heroic' era of the union's history, but far from the end of its story. One of the most important parts of this book is its account of how the union, both its officials and its rank-and-file, kept going through the grim years of the late 1920s and early 1930s. Even in perhaps the darkest hour, when the Labour movement was betrayed and divided by Ramsay MacDonald (who he greatly admired) George never faltered, staying true to his party and to the Union he founded. This is not the stuff of high drama, but it will be desperately familiar to anyone who lived through those times, or indeed others, when to be a trade unionist or a socialist was a hard and bitter fight.

Through all this George Edwards (Sir George as he became in 1930) kept his religious faith. Even this was not easy. The radical chapel of his youth had, by the 1900s, become a much more respectable and even conservative force. In this situation many members began to attack George for his Sunday union meetings and for his preaching of a steadfastly social gospel of Christ the carpenter. Occasionally, this also led him into conflict elsewhere as with the high church rector of Fakenham, the account of which is told in Chapter 10.

When Sir George Edwards died in 1933 the union he had founded was on a secure footing. Although it never contained the majority of farm workers nationally it did in the county of his birth. When I first came to the county to work on the union's history in 1974 I asked the then county organiser of the Union which areas of Norfolk were weak in union members. His reply was simple. Pointing to a map, covered with red-pins marking union branches, he said 'None'.

To end this brief introduction I would like to say something about the book and its author, a remarkable man in his own right. Noel Edwards, was George Edward's adopted son. His mother, a widow, cared for George in his later years, and, being childless, he adopted Noel, who then took his name.

Like his father, Noel Edwards is a working man. He began life as a printer, serving his apprenticeship in Fakenham. Also like his father he was a Labour man and a deeply committed Christian. It was this belief that lead to him becoming a conscientious objector during the Second World War. By 'daring to be a Daniel', Noel, like many christians and socialists before him, risked everything for his beliefs. He was sacked from his work, because the other printers would not work with him. He was married with a baby girl. After some months of unemployment he found work as an agricultural storekeeper at a local garage, staying there for the duration of the war, and serving with the ARP. After the war he went to work in Kent, first with a horticultural nurseryman, and then back at his old trade of printing. In the 1950s he returned to Norfolk and to the firm in Fakenham where he had served his apprenticeship. He kept in that employment until his retirement in 1979. Throughout his life he has been an active trade unionist and socialist, serving as the local Labour Party Secretary, in which capacity he founded, in 1946, the Fakenham Trades Council. After his return to Norfolk he became active in local politics having served on the Town Council for twenty-three years (for a period with his wife), the County Council for five years and the District Council for twenty-seven years. He has been a Methodist local preacher for over sixty years.

The book also has a remarkable history. As Noel writes in his Introduction, George Edwards himself wrote his autobiography up to his election to Parliament in 1920. This was published as *From Crow Scaring to Westminster* in 1922. During his later years he was asked to up date it but never did. Instead he asked Noel to carry out the task for him, which eventually he did. I first heard of the manuscript in 1983 when I was involved in the exhibition at the Norfolk Rural Life Museum on the history of the land workers' unionism in Norfolk which was held to mark the fiftieth anniversary of George's death. At that time because of other pressures I did nothing but in 1995, having been asked to write an entry on George for the new *Dictionary of National Biography*, I contacted Noel.

I came away with the manuscript, and the sad history of his failure to get it published. I was particularly angered by the insensitivity and arrogance of some academics who had dismissed the account as being of little worth since it did not meet 'academic' standards as social history. Reading the biography, I felt most strongly it should be published, not only as a biography of an important trade unionist but also because it was in itself a valuable piece of working class culture. The fact that its title, consciously or unconsciously, echoes Bunyan's *Pilgrims Progress* speaks volumes. Noel Edwards' book stands firmly in that line which runs from the great writing of English popular nonconformity in the seventeenth and eighteenth centuries, through to the memoirs of the working men and women who created the labour movement in the late nineteenth and twentieth. Tragically, it probably stands at the end of that line. There are a number of reasons for this. Partly it is that the huge changes in our culture since the Second World War have rendered this kind of project obsolete. Perhaps more importantly, the labour movement, which George Edwards helped make, has changed. It lacks both the conviction and the certainty in human progress that it once possessed. Sadly, I cannot believe that the Labour Party of our day has much time for the passionate christian belief in progress coupled with the unswerving loyalty to their class which characterised not only the life of George Edwards but that of tens of thousands of working men and women of his generation. If you want to see what I mean, turn to the last chapter of this book and see George Edwards, barely a fortnight before his death, aged eighty-three, arguing on Walsingham Board of Guardians that something should be done to help a land worker and his family threatened with eviction from a tied house. Some of George Edward's story is well enough known, especially to those, increasingly few in number I suspect, who have read his own account in *Crow Scaring to Westminster*. That book covers the 'heroic' period of the first unions of the 1870s and the 1900s. His life after the early 1920s is less well known, and probably less exciting. Yet it remains very important. It shows him in his last years, beset by illness and difficulty but refusing to give up. It may lack the drama of the pioneer years but it is a moving and powerful account of a life.

Noel's life of his father ends with a verse and I would like to end my introduction with one. It is one with which George was familiar, as was his whole generation, and one which speaks for them.

> Standing by a purpose true,
> Heeding God's command.
> Honour them, the faithful few,
> Hail to Daniel's Band.
> Dare to be a Daniel,
> Dare to stand alone.
> Dare to have a purpose firm,
> Dare to make it known.

Notes

1. *Eastern Weekly Press*, 22 June 1872.
2. Wages are difficult to work out, especially since they varied so much from county to county. These are based on my work and on W.A. Armstrong, *Farmworkers: A Social and Economic History 1770-1980* (London 1988).
3. *Eastern Weekly Press*, 10 October 1873.

Further Reading.

If you want to know more about the background to this book you could look at some of the following. My own book *Poor Labouring Men: Rural Radicalism in Norfolk, 1870-1923,* (1985) published by Routledge tells the history of the trades unions in some detail. On the chapels and unionism, Nigel Scotland, *Methodism and the Revolt of the Field in East Anglia,* (1981) published by Alan Sutton is good. More generally on the chapel and its world Norma Virgoe and Tom Williamson, *Religious Dissent in East Anglia,* (1993) published by the Centre of East Anglian Studies, UEA, has interesting material as does Steve Cherry's history of the Norwich Labour movement *Doing Different?* (1989) also published by the Centre.

Chapter 1

Childhood and Youth

The lives of George Edwards' parents are difficult to recover. His mother, Mary, had her roots in Norfolk. She married Robert Stageman by whom she had three children. The conditions of life then prevailing must have been the contributory factors of Robert's death from tuberculosis (then known as consumption). With no one left to support her and her children, she was compelled to seek the meagre sustenance which the local poor law institution of the day had to offer. It was quite probable that it was whilst she was there that she met Thomas Edwards, George Edwards's father.

The forebears of Thomas Edwards remain obscure, probably because their origin was in Wales. Edwards being a Welsh name, one can presume that one of them could well have been a drover who, as custom was, brought sheep from Wales, Scotland and the North of England to Norfolk's annual sheep fairs and sales. This custom continued up to the first quarter of the twentieth century. Quite likely therefore, one of Thomas Edwards' ancestors did this and finally settled in Norfolk.

Thomas Edwards was an experienced agricultural worker who had left that work to join the army. He served with the 60th Rifles and was sent overseas to fight in the Spanish Civil War of 1823 in the interests of Queen Isabel. He completed ten years' service with an exemplary record and character. Returning to his home at Marsham, the little Norfolk village ten miles from Norwich and one and a half miles from Aylsham, he found, rather than being welcomed as a hero, he was looked upon as a criminal. He had been deprived of the £9 bounty that, on his enlistment in the army he had been promised when his service was completed. Without a penny to his name, he now found himself denied work simply because he had been a soldier (a profession in those days looked upon with distrust as with people of low character or criminals).

He was not alone in being without work, there were many in his village in the same predicament. On 6 November 1833, a meeting was held in the village to call attention to their plight and demand work and food. The meeting was opened by the repeating of the Lord's Prayer.

There followed heated words with a resolution moved by Thomas Edwards demanding work and better wages. To this was added the words, 'The labourer is worthy of his hire'. A farmer present, angry at what he saw and heard, shouted to Thomas: 'You can go and pick blackberries or starve, you'll have no work from me'. Not long afterwards Thomas found this threat a reality. No work or food was available and he went into the fields and picked blackberries to eat. The very same farmer that had shouted at him at the meeting, caught him and turned him off the field. With no work, food or money he, too, was compelled to seek shelter at Buxton (near Aylsham) workhouse. It was just before Christmas, and he stayed there throughout the winter.

1. Sir George Edward's birthplace at Marsham Norfolk, with Sir George standing in the doorway. c.1920.

Thomas and Mary Edwards began their married life in a little cottage at Marsham in a lane a few yards from the main Aylsham to Norwich Road. The cottage still stands, now completely modernised, only its front remains in its original form with the adjoining cottage. Until its modernisation in the 1970s, two red bricks at the rear of the cottage remained with Mary's name and '1859' still clearly decipherable.

It was here on 5 October 1850 that Mary gave birth to her last child, George, later christened in the parish church. The family now consisted of six children, including the three from her first marriage.

With every addition to their family, Thomas and Mary found their poverty increased, for work and food were still scarce, wages low and hours of labour long. Thomas, after leaving the workhouse, had obtained work for the summer as a brick maker. Then, when that was finished, he obtained work as a cattle-feeder at eight shillings per week. But by the time George was born wages had been reduced to seven shillings per week for married men and five shillings per week for single men. Upon the noble sum of seven shillings, Thomas was expected to keep his wife and six children. The price of a 4lb loaf was one and sixpence. The bakers were not allowed to offer for sale any bread until it had been baked at least twenty-four hours. Rice and other substitutes were extensively used to stave off famine. This was the true economic fact of life for them, despite the repeal of the Corn Laws which hitherto had helped to increase the cost of living. The result was that Mary, confined to bed with her babe, George, was forced to live on onion gruel (onions boiled with and thickened by flour, with dripping, salt and pepper added).

When George was one week old, Mary found she was no longer able to breast feed him. She had to feed him upon bread soaked in skimmed milk. In face of their extreme poverty and personal suffering through the lack of many of the essentials to life, it was a wonder how they survived. But they did and were able to bring their family up. George in particular continued to grow in strength. In order to add to the earnings of her husband, Mary worked at the old village industry of hand-loom weaving. This domestic village industry, in common with other industries of that day, was a sweated one. It entailed being at the loom sixteen hours per day in order to ensure a wage of four shillings a week.

When George was four years old, in 1854, the Crimean War began. This added further to the miseries of the working-classes. Food again rose to famine prices. Thomas Edwards was at this time working as a bullock feeder. His hours were from daylight to dark. His wages were four shillings short of the sum required to provided the family with bread. To counteract this, each night on his way home from work he would fill his lunch bag with turnips from his employer's field. These

Mary would boil for the children's supper. Many a time little George saw his parents faint through fatigue and the lack of proper food. Every hour of the day and far into the night they were toiling to provide the wherewithal for their family. Mother washing and mending the clothes which had to be worn over and over again (their poverty preventing them possessing any more to change into), father mending and shining the boots. Harriet assisted Mother during the day in hand-loom weaving. The eldest son, Joseph, at this time twelve years old, was working for one shilling and two pence per week. Two of the stepsons, being fortunate enough to have been left a little money by an uncle, had been apprenticed into the carpentry and joinery trade. The third stepson had gone to sea. George experienced his first taste of real distress when he was five years old. One night his father, coming home as usual from work with his nightly rations of turnips, was stopped by a policemen and searched. Upon finding him in possession of his employer's turnips he was immediately escorted to the police station. He was not allowed to see his wife and family first. They were anxiously awaiting his return with their supper. His non-arrival meant they had to go to bed hungry. The next day Thomas Edwards was brought before the magistrate charged with stealing from his employer. He was sentenced to fourteen days hard labour.

Deprived of their bread-winner, Mary and her family were compelled to enter the workhouse. They were taken there in a cart by the relieving officer. Little George, rather frightened at having to leave his home, lagged behind. The officer, angry and impatient at being kept waiting, seized him and threw him into the cart. This at once aroused within the mother's heart the hidden fire of resentment which up to then she had bravely kept under control. She immediately jumped up and slapped the officer's face. Upon arrival at the workhouse, she was punished for this by being separated from her baby boy and forced to pick oakum.

Upon his release, Thomas Edwards found himself denied work because of his prison sentence. With no alternative, he also had to enter the workhouse. Here, he and his family had to stay until the following spring when he was fortunate in obtaining employment as a brick maker in Alby, a little village seven-and-a-half miles from Marsham. At this work he was away all the week. He earned four shillings for every thousand bricks he made, having in the process to run the clay three

2. Sir George Edward's parents, Thomas and Mary Edwards.

times. With the aid of one of his sons he was enabled to take home thirteen shillings per week. This came as a godsend to Mary. The Crimean War had brought an end to the industry of handloom weaving, and so she herself was unable to earn any extra money by that means.

In March 1856, George, not yet six years old, became a wage-earner, his first job being to scare crows. Soon after sunrise he started his day's work in a neighbouring farmer's field. He would shout loudly 'car-woo-car-woo-wooh-wooh' and run about waving a stick with which to further frighten the birds from the corn. This work, and work it was for one so young, was continued until sunset when the birds had gone to roost. Then he was allowed to go home.

What a proud chappie he was when he received his first week's wage of one whole shilling. He ran home as fast as his little legs could carry him. Proudly he presented his mother, whom he loved so dearly, with the shilling. With the memory so fresh of his mother's tears on so many occasions, and of the brutal treatment of his father, he said: 'Mother, this is my money. Now we shall not want bread any more, and you will not have to cry again. You shall always have my money, I will always look after you'.[1] One day, the crows seemed extra hungry. George was kept continually on the run. His little limbs ached so much that at last, sitting himself down intending only to have a minute's rest, he fell fast asleep. The farmer caught hold of the poor child and soundly thrashed him. Not satisfied with this cruel punishment to a child so young, he deducted two pence from George's wages at the end of the week. This left him with only ten pence to take home to his mother. Feeling very crestfallen, he held out the money to her. Broken-heartedly he told her all about it. Mary did not scold him, but comforted him with the words that better days were ahead - a prophesy she was partly to see fulfilled in her day.

When the crow-scaring season finished, George was given the job of looking after the cows, seeing that they did not get out of the fields, then taking them back to be milked in the evening. This work he did until the harvest commenced. Then, with other little boys of the village he made bonds for the women who were employed to tie up the corn which the men had mowed with the scythe. Mechanisation had not at this period become established on the land. For this work George and his comrades were paid three pence per day (one shilling and sixpence per week).

The corn being cut and ready for carting, George was then employed as a 'Hold-jee Boy'. This job was to ride upon the horse's back, warn the men on top of the loaded corn on the wagon that the horse was about to be moved. This the boys did by shouting 'Hold-jee' ('Hold tight'). Once the corn was carted it was the custom in those days to allow the poor to glean the fragments. In this way they were often able to glean enough to provide them with bread for the winter months. The men folk would thresh the gleanings with a flail, dress it and clean it. It would then be sent to the mill where it was ground into meal of which the bread would be made.

After the harvest of 1856 George left his employer, having obtained work at a farm owned by a man named Thomas Whighton. Here he was given the job of looking after the cows and also scaring crows when the wheat had been sown. When winter came George cleaned turnips. It was a cold, back-aching job for an adult, but for a child of six years it was cruelty indeed. His only breakfast was bread soaked in boiling water (with a small piece of butter added when possible as a special treat). For dinner he had two slices of bread, a small piece of cheese with an apple or an onion. Mr Whighton was a very hard man. George received many thrashings from him when he did not clean as many turnips as was expected of him.

Between the years 1858 to 1869 George experienced many changes of employment. Among these were brick making with his father, horse-keeping and ploughing. He had soon learned to do the many skilled jobs to be done upon a farm. His pride at becoming efficient enough to plough at the age of ten years, however, was rather cruelly shattered. The old farm steward, who was noted for being a tyrant, rode up to George one day. He accused him of not ploughing straight enough and smote him across the knuckles with his riding whip. George's spirit rose defiantly. He swore at the steward and called him a liar. The steward got from his horse, took George across his knee and thrashed him until he was black with bruises, but not without himself having become severely kicked by George in the process. His mother hearing of this immediately went after the steward. She soundly slapped his face and pulled his beard. It resulted in her being summoned before the magistrate. She was given the alternative of paying a five-shilling fine or serving a prison sentence of fourteen days hard labour. The fine was paid by a kind friend.

Much against his mother's wishes, George left home when he was sixteen. He accepted work as a team-man for a farmer at Docking, a village about thirty miles from Marsham in the King's Lynn/Hunstanton area of the county. However, George did not feel at home there as he felt he was being treated like a foreigner, so he only stayed there one year. Upon returning to his home he obtained work upon a farm in Marsham. Here he lived in the farmhouse and received a weekly wage of two shillings. Board and lodging was provided.

An unfortunate incident ended this employment. One day George and his mate were ploughing when their employer came to them and accused them of having wasted time by stopping at the end of the field. George denied this and called the farmer a liar, adding a few choice words in rather stronger language. The farmer smote him with his clenched fist and knocked George down. Quickly getting to his feet George returned the blow and his mate lent his weight to the struggle. The result was, of course, that George had again to seek another job. This time he obtained work on a brick field in the neighbouring village of Bessingham.

3. Sir George, a ploughboy aged seventeen with his mother, 1867.

The first nineteen years of George's life had brought him much physical suffering. He had experienced several changes of employment. The years had not contained much in the way of pleasure or recreation for him. The only avenue open to him when he was free from the daily toil was the public house. This he had begun to visit. He never got the worse for drink, but he joined in some of the wild games of other young people he met there and acquired some of their habits and foul language. He also joined the ranks of the poachers.

The wildness of the young people seemed to reach its height upon the occasion of St Valentine's night (14 February) and Guy Fawkes' night (5 November). Upon the former they would play all manner of tricks upon the village folks who might be quietly sitting by their fires when one of the youths would knock upon the door. He would be dressed in a top hat, and long coat. Through the top and sides of the top hat pins would have been stuck. Following much knocking and banging upon the door, and tapping upon the window with a button fixed to elastic, the tenant would come angrily to the door. All but the lad in the top hat would run away. The angry tenant would raise his hand to smite the lad of the head and would be sorely pricked by the pins. Many similar and wilder pranks were played.

On Guy Fawkes' night they would make their fun and games around a huge fire in one of the fields or on common land. Upon one such occasion George and his mates had got a good fire going when a farmer came up and was very interested in the fire they had. He said, 'That's a good blaze, my boys, go and get some more sticks.' This they did, when they were nearly burnt he said 'Good, go and get some more, let's have a real blaze'. He must have been drunk, for the sticks were his own which he had stored in his barn for thatching (called 'Broaches' and pronounced 'Brorches' by Norfolk people). The farmer found this out in his sober hours the next day. Unfortunately, too late, for all had been taken at his own request, and he did not know who the lads were.

George's poaching activities, however, were more profitable in that he was able to sell the game for pocket money with which to buy his drink and tobacco. For he had become a heavy pipe-smoker and his small wage at that time left little for pleasure after he had given what he could to his mother.

In 1869 his latest change of employment was accompanied by another experience which was to alter the whole course of his life. It was one which brought about by what he said in later years to have been 'the spiritual forces coming into contact with the forces of evil, which up till then were completely controlling my life.'[2] Added to this, no doubt, was the realisation within himself that his habits and the company he was keeping, was causing grave anxiety to his mother who was such a saintly, god-fearing woman. George was deeply conscious of her wonderful love and sacrifice for her family. He had no wish ever knowingly to add extra burden and suffering upon her.

It happened on a Sunday when George chanced to be passing the village Methodist Chapel, and decided to go in. A very sincere local preacher, by the name of Samuel Harrison, was preaching. His text was, 'How shall we escape if we neglect so great a salvation?' (2 Heb. 3). It was quite an orthodox evangelistic sermon of the time but the message touched George's conscience and heart, for he had listened intently, although fighting a rebellion within himself. It led him to confess his evil ways and to become converted to the way of Christ. From then onward he gave up his visits to the public house, attending regularly instead the Primitive Methodist Chapel, of which he soon became a member, no longer a poacher, but a faithful follower of Jesus Christ.

In the spring of 1870 George made a further change of employment. He obtained work at a brick field in the village of Alby. Here he had yet another experience which was still further to affect his future life. George met and fell in love with Charlotte Corke, a young woman living close to the brick field where he was working. Charlotte, the youngest of a family of nine, like George, had felt the pangs of hunger and poverty. But, unlike him, she had been fortunate in being able to attend a Dame School where she, amongst other useful things, had learned the three 'R's' (reading, writing and arithmetic).

It was not long before these two young people became engaged. They were married at Alby Church on 21 June 1872. Charlotte immediately began the task of teaching George to read and write. He had become very keenly sensitive of his illiteracy after his conversion to christianity, especially as it had brought him the call to become a local preacher. The Aylsham primitive methodist church circuit quarterly meeting had given him a Note of Liberty. This permitted him to take part in the conduct of worship in the company of two accredited local preachers, Edward Gladden and James Applegate. After two quarters in their company the circuit quarterly meeting agreed that his name should appear on their full plan of accredited preachers, and he was soon after allowed to take his own services.

The preparation for his first service was quite an ordeal for him. Not yet having fully accomplished the art of reading and writing, he had, with the aid of Charlotte, to commit to memory three hymns and a bible passage. This was the first chapter of St John. He had also to memorise his sermon. The method Charlotte used to help George in learning his hymns and bible passages was to read the lines out to him and he would repeat them after her until the whole was instilled into his mind.

The day for his first preaching appointment arrived. Accompanied by Charlotte, he set off feeling rather nervous. In those days the preacher read out the hymns two lines at a time. In this way the congregation were able to remember the lines. They, like George, were so often those that had no education. There would also be a tune-starter amongst the congregation, because they did not have a musical instrument in the little village chapels at that time. Should there not be a tune-starter present, then the preacher would have to do that himself. On that first occasion, much to George's relief, he found there was a tune-starter present for his first service. His hymns were all real old ranter hymns: 'Hark the gospel news is sounding,' 'Stop poor sinner, stop and think before you further go,' and 'There is a fountain filled with blood drawn from Emmanuel's veins'. His text was 'Behold the Lamb of God which taketh away the sins of the world' (St John I v. 29).

From this time onward George made great progress in his education. The ability to read having been accomplished, his yearning for knowledge increased. The only two books he possessed as yet, however, were his Bible and hymn book. George was, nevertheless, quite determined to save what he could in order gradually to procure more. With this end in view he gave up smoking. This was a great sacrifice for him to make, although he did not smoke as much as he had previous to his conversion, he was still very fond of his pipe. For a long time George was seen with a small twig in his mouth, which he found gradually enabled him to do away with his pipe altogether.

His smoking money saved, he was enabled to purchase several books quite cheaply through the kindness of his friend, James Applegate. George was thus able to build up a small library of which he made full use and was justifiably proud. Often in his later days, upon the occasions when he entertained his colleagues and friends, when asked by them to join them in a smoke, he would take them and show them his bookshelves lined with books and say: 'this is my Tobacco'. When I was a child I acted as a child, but when I became a man I put away childish things.' This bit of dry humour was always taken in the true spirit in which it was given.

George spent many hours studying his books. Soon he became a powerful and convincing preacher. He had the joy of seeing many of his hearers converted to a better way of life. Some later returned from far-away places and thanked him for his help and guidance in their earlier years. However, not only did George's studies of the scriptures prove instrumental in his becoming an able preacher, but also brought him to the view that the conditions of life around him were contrary to the way of Christ. His outlook broadened. Christianity came to mean for him something more than the 'saving of souls' and the overcoming of personal sin. He saw it now as a means of improving the moral and social standard of the whole of life. Instrumental in bringing him to this school of thought were the great social injustices experienced by his parents during his childhood. Experiences which as he said in later years, 'became branded within me like as it were with a red hot iron'. The sum total of this was that he became determined to do all within his power to improve the conditions of life for his fellowmen.

Notes

1.   George Edwards, *From Crow Scaring to Westminster* (London, 1922), p.23.
2.   Edwards, *Crow Scaring* p.29.

Chapter 2

Union Man

During the year 1872 the whole countryside was seething with discontent. Although the general improvement of agriculture brought with it a slight rise in the standard of life of the worker, conditions in rural England were far from being what they should. The workers were still compelled to work very long hours. Fear of victimisation prevented them asking for any increase in their meagre wages. Things began to look very serious. It was at this time, with the knowledge that the town workers were already organised into unions, that the rural workers felt that they too should become organised. In this way they believed they also would be better able to command an improvement in their lot. With this end in view, Joseph Arch, a primitive methodist local preacher of Barford in Warwickshire, had been approached to take the lead. This he agreed to do. This move on the part of the agricultural workers was heralded by the Norfolk press as 'the Uprising of the Agricultural Labourer'.

A meeting of the union was called at Alby where George was then working. It was addressed by another local preacher by the name of Josiah Mills. George attended the meeting, during the course of which he was pointed out to the speaker as one who had suffered much at the hands of the farming community. He was invited to relate his experiences. Following the meeting he realised the movement offered him an opportunity to fulfil his vow to work for the improvement of his fellow men. He became a union man, joining the local union and pledging to give it his wholehearted support.

As the unions in Norfolk grew a meeting was arranged for Joseph Arch at Aylsham to try and bring all the local Norfolk unions together. It was at this meeting that George first met Joseph Arch and through it came to know Zacharias Walker who was seven years older than he. Zach Walker was the son of a primitive methodist minister, the Revd James Walker. Zach had the advantage of an education through his parents. He remained a firm and faithful colleague of Joseph Arch despite the divisions among the labourers. He did valiant work with Arch's union until its collapse in the 1890s. However, although George, Joseph Arch and Zach Walker were called to work for a common cause they were destined to do it in the camps of rival unions because the Norfolk workers in George's area were not greatly impressed by Arch's union. It was decided by a majority vote to continue as they were in separate district unions. Both George and Joseph felt very disappointed by this decision. They both considered it a grave mistake. The future unhappily proved them right. Nevertheless George always worked closely and in harmony with Zach Walker. When the District and Parish Council Bill of 1894 was brought in they 'jointly entered into a campaign during the passage of the Bill through Parliament'.[1]

George himself was soon made aware of what it meant to be a union man. In the year 1873 great stimulus had been given to the workers' unions by their demand for a two shillings wage increase being granted. This brought their wages from eleven to thirteen shillings per week. The following year it was considered a further demand for an increase of two shillings per week, with the addition of time off for breakfast, should be made. But the demand was not acceded to without a struggle. One of the bitterest opponents of it was George's employer, James Ryce. George was involved in the strike that followed. He had the brick making trade to fall back upon so did not depend upon union support. He was offered work in that trade by his old friend, James Applegate at Oulton near Alysham. Following the conceding of the men's demands, wholesale dismissals followed where men refused to give up their union card. But the union's power was greatly weakened just as Joseph Arch and George had feared by their own divisions. Many lost interest and migrated to better conditions.

In October 1879, George left Oulton, and his old friend James Applegate, to take up employment as a brick maker for Mr Cook of Twaite Hall near Alby. He and Charlotte moved into part of the farmhouse. The condition of this employment was that he should take work by contract, raise the earth, make the bricks and burn them, the rate to be ten shillings per thousand, the employer to find all tools and coal. When not so engaged the employer agreed to find him work as a farm worker. As such he could do a harvest.

Although so many workers had now lost interest in the unions, George did not do so. He had in this latest move left the area of the union to which he had belonged so he immediately joined Arch's union, in whose area he now resided. He soon became an active member of it. This did not appear to upset George's new employer. He continued to get on well with him for quite a long time until in 1885 he involved himself in a campaign which was sponsored by the Liberal Party for the granting to the agricultural worker the franchise. When the Franchise Bill was eventually brought before the House of Commons by Mr Gladstone, then Prime Minister, it was bitterly opposed by the Tories. Unfortunately George's employer was a true dyed-in-the-wool Tory. Hearing of George's involvement in the campaign, he sent for George and informed him that he would not have any man of his attending or addressing such campaign meetings. Such behaviour he considered was setting class against class. To which George replied that as much as he respected Mr Cook as his employer he respected his own liberty a great deal more. He would not under any condition comply with Mr Cook's request. Further, he added, he considered so long as he did his work satisfactorily and did not neglect it in any way, and lived an honest, straightforward life, neither Mr Cook nor anyone else had any right to dictate how he was to spend his evenings. He considered that he had a right to this freedom as a free citizen.

Cook could find no answer to this, but said he must leave his employ. George's whole being revolted against this threat, but he answered quietly in accepting his notice. Apparently this rather took his employer by surprise, for he then asked George when he required his notice to expire. George replied. 'Not until I have finished my contract. I have already raised sufficient earth to make one hundred thousand bricks which I shall finish before I leave.' Cook argued that he would compel him to leave at once. George invited him to try, adding: 'If you do I will sue you for breach of contract'. Realising what the consequences might be if he gave George the chance to sue him, Cook gave in. He asked him to finish his contract first.

Nevertheless, Cook, finding himself beaten in this instance, sought and found another meaner way of hitting back at him. He was a member of the Board of Guardians to whom George's mother-in-law, then living with George, had to apply for relief. He was instrumental in getting sixpence per week deducted from her allowance. George at once informed the leaders of his union and those of the local Liberal Party. As a result his victimisation became very widely known. It was denounced from every platform in the county where franchise for the workers was being demanded. As can be expected, this caused great consternation in the local Tory camp. The Liberal Party offered George a job as an organiser, but he turned it down. He insisted that he desired to finish his contract so as not to give his employer the opportunity to get behind him through having himself broken it.

Once the Franchise Bill was passed granting the agricultural workers a vote for the first time in history, it soon became evident that a general

31

election would not long be delayed. Norfolk was mapped out into six single-seat constituencies. The district in which George lived was placed in the North Norfolk constituency.

With the approach of the end of George's contract and the termination of his employment, necessitating also the removal from his home, a tied dwelling, it was also apparent to the local Tories that it would coincide with the general election. Realising the awkward position this would place them in from the point of view of its propaganda value to their opponents, they advised Cook to withdraw his notice. He did so. This was considered by the local Liberals and trade union leaders as a victory. But George himself did not feel too happy about it. He was sure that once the election was over his employer would find some excuse to get rid of him.

In October 1885 the election campaign began. George went into action. His evenings were spent addressing meetings in support of the Liberal candidate, Mr Herbert Cozens-Hardy (later Lord Cozens-Hardy, Master of the Rolls and, by a strange coincidence, the father of the man who was later to be George's own opponent in his first bid for parliamentary honours). The Liberal Party were successful in this election, Cozens-Hardy being elected for North Norfolk. Joseph Arch, who had stood for North-West Norfolk, was also successful.

At the beginning of 1886, George found his premonition concerning his employer's intentions was about to be fulfilled. When he asked for his orders with regard to brick making, he was informed that due to there being so many standing on the ground and the brick-sale having decreased, it was not intended to make any more that year. George, however, knew that in fact the truth was there were not so many bricks standing by twenty thousand in comparison with the previous year when his employer had given him the contract to make a hundred thousand. Also George knew the selling prospects were greater than the previous year. It was only a question of a few weeks after this that he received notice terminating his employment and giving him six months in which to find another house. After searching miles for work and a home, George was eventually successful in obtaining a season's brick-making for a Mr Emery of Stibbard. It was not until 11 October, the day he had to quit his house, that he was able through the kindness of a friend, a Mr Carr of Wickmere, to find alternative accommodation. No one would employ or let a house to him when it became known that he was an active union man and one who had actively supported the Liberal Party. He was branded as an agitator.

July 1886 saw the downfall of Gladstone's Government over the Irish Home Rule Bill which caused a split in his own party. Once more George was in the forefront in the election which followed. This time the Liberals were defeated. The Tories were returned to power with grave consequences for George and his fellow agricultural workers. The local employers began to play havoc with the known trade unionists.

George, having completed his season's work at Stibbard, was amongst many who found difficulty in obtaining other work. Trade unionism in Norfolk soon became completely disrupted and almost petered out. Eventually, after many weeks of unemployment and uncertainty, he was offered work by Mr Ketton, a Liberal, of Felbrigg Hall, near Cromer. This was six miles from where he was then living at Wickmere. Mr Ketton took him on as a labourer. He paid him one shilling per week above the standard rate at that time. But not until eighteen months later was this employer able to offer him a house. During this period George had thus to walk 12 miles a day to and from work. However, he felt himself compensated by the fact that Mr Ketton was particularly kind to him by giving him every opportunity to earn extra money and he never interfered with George's leisure hour activities. Once again he was enabled to settle down to a quieter life. He had a good job and a decent home. He spent most of his evenings studying religious and political books, having now completely mastered the art of reading and writing through the continued help of Charlotte his wife.

Notes

1.   Edwards *Crow Scaring,* p.66.

Chapter 3

Union Organiser and Local Councillor

It was the fifth of November 1889, when George was sitting by the fire at home with Charlotte, studying his books, that there was a knock upon the door. Opening it, wondering who it could be at that time, he found a deputation of eleven men who said they represented a large number of others who desired to re-form the union. They would like him to lead them. George felt greatly tempted to refuse the request. He had now at last been able to settle down with Charlotte to enjoy a more peaceful existence than hitherto. To consent to the request he knew would mean again plunging into public work of the sort that would invite victimisation and hardship.

It was not easy to reach the right decision. Joseph Arch's union was practically defunct in Norfolk at this time. The men therefore expressed their wish to form a union upon the lines of the Federal Union which was organised by a Mr Rix of Swanton Morley, near East Dereham. This was a breakaway union from that of Mr Arch's.

After listening to the men, he pointed out what the cost of attempting to re-form the union might mean to them. But they convinced him of their sincerity and he agreed to help them. But he emphasised that it would be, in his opinion, useless if they made their sole aim merely the raising of wages. George told them, 'we must aim high, endeavouring not merely to increase wages, but to improve the social and moral conditions of rural life, creating thereby a better spirit between master and man'.

After the deputation had left, George at once put away his books. He wrote to Mr Rix suggesting that he attend meetings at Cromer and Aylmerton to explain the rules and objects of his union. To this suggestion he agreed and, with George, addressed two crowded meetings at these places. The result being that a union was formed which was named The Norfolk and Norwich Federal Union, Cromer District. Its rules and objects were to:

1. Improve the social and moral well-being of its members.

2. To assist members to secure allotments and representation upon local authorities and in parliament.

3. To assist members to migrate and emigrate.

4. Ten shillings per week to be paid as strike and victimisation pay.

5. Legal advice to be given.

6. Each member to pay one shilling levy per harvest to enable a member to have his harvest money made up in the event of dispute.

7. A contribution of nine pence per week to be made, eight pence of which to be allocated to district funds and one penny to be retained for local branch management.

George was unanimously elected honorary district secretary. In a year's strenuous work of organising numerous new branches within a radius of ten to twelve miles, he enroled over a thousand members. To get to and from these places he had to walk, there being no other means of travel available for him. At the first district annual meeting of the union, George reported upon his year's work and the progress made. It was decided, in view of the great work he had done in advancing the membership, that he should be made a full-time organiser, at a salary of one pound per week. Under such pressure he reluctantly agreed, but adamantly insisted that he should receive only fifteen shillings per week. He pointed out that the workers themselves were only receiving ten shillings per week.

It was not long before his strength and willpower in his new capacity was put to the test. He had made up his mind to do all he could to avoid strikes, but as time went by it became very evident that this would be impossible. Trouble developed in the village of Hindolveston, about sixteen or seventeen miles from George's home. Here a farmer locked his men out, having ordered them to cut meadow grass at the rate of three and sixpence per acre. The men rejected the terms. They called George in to mediate on their behalf. Upon arrival at the farmer's house he found him a most arrogant and belligerent man. He ordered George off the premises, threatening to put his dog upon him if he should attempt to set foot upon his land again. To this threat George replied that he had come expecting to deal with a gentleman, but found to his regret that it was with a man who was not sufficiently intelligent to treat another with respect. He added, 'in less than a week you will send for me, on which occasion I will show you the respect that is now lacking in you.' These words proved true. As the days went by this farmer came to realise how determined the men were to stand firm for their rights. He endeavoured to make terms with them, but they refused and referred him to George. He was therefore compelled within a week to send for him. After this meeting with George the farmer agreed to pay the men five shillings per acre. The dispute was settled and the men returned to work.

This dispute was shortly followed by another, this time at Great Plumstead, near Norwich. The men demanded a shilling wage increase, but this strike proved to be of a more serious nature, a hundred men being involved. It was further complicated by the fact that the Farmers' Federation were able to find several men to fill the places of those on strike. More than a month passed without a settlement, but at last George's zeal and tact was rewarded, the men's spirits were kept up. Their loyalty and steadfastness won them the day. The shilling increase was granted.

Nevertheless dark days were once more looming ahead for George and his fellow workers. The years 1891-92 brought depression to agriculture. The farmers combined in demanding a general wage reduction. The Federal Union, of which George was organiser, united with that of Arch's union to resist this demand. Great was the bitterness over this prolonged struggle. Unemployment and evictions became numerous again throughout the villages in the whole countryside. The spirits of the men were at last broken. They were forced to accept defeat and resumed work at the reduced rates offered them.

In these hard times many men felt compelled to forsake the unions. But George and a few of his loyal colleagues in the Federal Union did not give up in despair. The second county council election in 1892 gave them an opportunity to bring to public notice the plight of the agricultural worker. The Cromer District of the Federal Union believed it was possible for them to win the seat for that area. In so doing they believed they would assure the workers were represented in the council chamber which, at that period, comprised only those representing farmers', landlords' and employers' interests.

George was requested by the union to allow himself to be nominated to contest the Cromer and District seat. It had hitherto been represented by Mr Bond Cabbell, a local landlord who had not previously been opposed. George accepted the invitation in the belief that not only would he receive the support of his union members, but also that of the local Liberals for whose cause he had already worked and suffered much for. Immediately following his nomination he was sadly disillusioned. The leading Liberal in the district nominated the Tory, Mr Bond Cabbell. Unfortunately this resulted in a campaign fought on class basis. George experienced great bitterness from his opponent's supporters. They inferred that he was impotent. It was made to appear a disgusting thing that a common labourer should dare to oppose a landlord and by so doing to judge himself more fit to serve upon that august body, the Norfolk County Council.

The constituency comprised fourteen parishes, covering roughly an area of seven to eight miles. George, unlike his opponent, had no means of travel other than his own two legs. He had therefore to walk to all his meetings. These he held in every place within the constituency. They were well attended and he received a good reception in the villages, but not so in Cromer, Sheringham and some of the larger villages where he was sometimes pelted with soot and flour by organised gangs of hooligans. He was ably helped and supported by Mr Henry Broadhurst, MP, and a loyal band of methodist local preachers and members of his union.

Towards the closing stages of the campaign some of his opponents published a cartoon depicting him lying in a coffin with Mr Broadhurst standing weeping by his side. Underneath was the caption 'Puzzle: find Edwards after the Election'. George felt very hurt by this action, especially as the publication of the cartoon followed closely upon the death of his mother. But he was very grateful that his opponent, Cabbell, strongly condemned those of his supporters who were responsible for the cartoon and even threatened to withdraw from the contest. It was a strange and sad thing that within three months of the election Mr Bond Cabell died.

The result of the poll was declared at Cromer Town Hall. It was:-

Bond Cabbell	505
George Edwards	455
Majority	50

The smallness of this majority was a shock for the Tories. They feared what the result of the next election might be, which came sooner than anticipated, due as has already been said, to the untimely death of Bond Cabbell. George's supporters again urged him to stand, but he felt it was too soon for him to do so again. His late employer, Mr Ketton, was nominated and returned unopposed.

However, George was not disheartened by his defeat. This was not the reason for his refusal to allow himself to be nominated for the by-election. He was of the opinion that his defeat was largely due to lack of organisation. But for that he felt the result would have been very different. This belief stirred him to greater activity to enrol more workers into the union. He was sure this would prove to be the key to the ultimate improvement of their lot. With this end in view, he walked hundreds of miles, seeing very little of his wife at home as a result. His efforts were rewarded by seeing several new branches added to the Cromer District of the Federal Union.

With the continued growth of the unions, the farmers became very alarmed. They once more resorted to the weapons of dismissal and eviction as a means to smash the unions. Both Arch's Union and that of the Federal Union became involved in strikes in several areas. This brought George and

Joseph together upon several occasions. They addressed numerous united meetings together, but the workers refused obstinately to take their advice and amalgamate into one union to strengthen their hand. In face of these trials, George felt himself powerless to help his fellow workers.

But there occurred an event in the midst of these troubles, in 1893, which enabled him to do much towards easing the burden of the poor. The Government, having appointed a Royal Commission to inquire into the administration of the Poor Law, invited George to give evidence before it in the Queen's Robing Room at the House of Lords. Amongst those appointed to serve on this Commission were the Prince of Wales (later King Edward VII), Lord Aberdare, the Rt Hon Joseph Chamberlain, Joseph Arch, MP, and Henry Broadhurst, MP. George, in his evidence, was able to prove the poorness of the quality of flour allowed by guardians. He produced some of their flour, together with some of the best flour one could buy. The contrast so greatly astonished the commission that they requested him to take both samples home and ask his wife to make two loaves of bread from it and to bring them before the commission the following week. When he did so, the difference in the quality of each loaf was even more pronounced than that seen previously between two kinds of flour.

Giving further evidence, George was asked about the treatment of the poor in his county. He instanced several cases of cruelty which he said was the common lot of the poor. Amongst these cases he described that of a widow with four children, one of whom was a young baby. She was allowed sixpence per week for each of the three children, but nothing for the baby. She was granted half a stone of flour for three but nothing for herself. George pointed out that a widow was supposed to keep herself and one child. This he told the commission was only a sample of the suffering these poor people were compelled to experience when forced to apply to the board of guardians for relief.

The position of the aged poor, he told them, was even worse than that of widows. They were allowed only one stone of flour and half-a-crown per week. George told how he had had to keep himself, his wife and his mother until the time of her death upon a wage of fifteen shillings per week, plus the noble sum of half-a-crown that was allowed her by the Aylsham board of guardians. The guardians refused to allow her any flour and further added to his poverty by compelling him to contribute one shilling and three pence per week towards the sum they had allowed. George was cross-examined by Mr Joseph Chamberlain. At the close, the late King Edward thanked George for the way in which he had presented his evidence. He added that he was deeply shocked to learn that the poor should have been treated in the manner shown by the evidence.

The publishing of the report of the Commission caused a great stir both in high places and in the country. Without a doubt it hastened the passing of the District and Parish Council Act of 1894 which provided for the establishment of a council in every parish having a population of 300 and over. These councils were given the power to provide allotments. It abolished all property qualifications in the election to the board of guardians.

No time was wasted by George or Joseph Arch's union organisers in preparing their members to stand as candidates in the forthcoming parish and district council elections in their areas. Although much bitter opposition was met with from landlords, farmers and certain clergy friends of theirs, the efforts of George and his colleagues bore fruit in some of the elections. They, including George and Charlotte, were elected to the Aylmerton and Felbrigg parish council. George was elected chairman at the first meeting of the council. They made their first job the provision of allotments for its parishioners. Next George and Charlotte, with other workers' representatives, tackled the district council elections. They were successful in being elected to the Erpingham district council. Of this council George remained a member for eighteen years and Charlotte remained a member for ten years.

Upon this council George and Charlotte lost no time in endeavouring to alter the standard of poor law relief then being administered. They were instrumental in bringing to light the many ways relieving officers were depriving the poor of relief. One such case was that of an aged widow whose relief had been stopped on the pretext that she had given birth to an illegitimate child. George and Charlotte were able to prove this to be false. The so-called illegitimate child was a married woman of thirty who had a child of her own. The relieving officer was severely reprimanded and was compelled to pay the poor widow all the back money due to her.

The next fight they had was over the quality of flour provided for the poor. On this occasion their efforts were strengthened by a Revd Carson. Both he and George had bread made from some of the flour meted out to the poor. This bread they each took with them to the council meeting. So poor in quality was the bread that it was found that the centre could be taken from the loaves quite easily, leaving the crust standing. The Revd Carson started the ball rolling by moving a resolution to the effect that the contractor who supplied the flour to the poor of the district should be named and brought to justice by having his name struck off the list of contractors. This caused great consternation amongst the council members. There were cries of

'Prove the flour is bad'. The Revd Carson pointed to his sample of bread. He asked the council whether or not they thought it fit for human consumption, whereupon a co-opted member of the council seized the bread and threw it upon the fire. This caused an uproar in the council chamber in which George, Charlotte and their colleagues took part. They loudly protested at the action of the co-opted member. In seconding Revd Carson's resolution, George challenged anyone to throw his sample of bread upon the fire. He said that he had also brought flour to prove the way in which the poor were being treated. He said that he was sure the poor of the district would appreciate the action the Revd Carson had courageously made in bringing the matter up. George further added that it was a disgrace that anyone in a christian country should produce such bread and flour for the poor.

After a heated debate, the co-opted member was forced to apologise for his action. The relieving officer revealed the fact that the board had put out its contract for the milling of the flour and allowed the contractor to sub-contract again. George and his colleagues protested against this kind of action. He said in so doing the board was encouraging a system which made a working-man the tool for someone else to sweat. It allowed, he said, that working-man in turn to put out the contract to someone else who again sweated another person. It was little wonder, therefore, that the final result was that the poor were provided with inferior bread. The outcome of it all was that George, Charlotte and their colleagues achieved a victory for the poor of their district in that no longer were they given flour as a form of relief but the equivalent in money.

The year 1895 began with the membership of the unions seriously depleted. George, in addition to his great fight on behalf of the poor upon the local councils, continued to exert all his strength to reorganise the workers. Several disputes broke out. Although he received help from the Land Restoration League, his efforts to keep the workers united and not to succumb to apathy had little effect. The drift from the unions continued. This was considerably hastened both by the weapons of dismissal and evictions used by the farmers and also by the reduction of wages to eleven shillings per week.

George and Charlotte endeavoured to meet this situation by further efforts on the district council. They proposed that the Council should hire fifty acres of land on which the unemployed could work. This move was defeated by the majority farmer-representation on the council. They then moved that the council's roadmen should be paid fifteen shillings per week. This was opposed on the grounds that it would cause further dissatisfaction to those employed on the land because the farmers said it was difficult enough for them to pay even eleven shillings per week. So George and Charlotte's efforts were again defeated.

Further disruption of the unions was caused with the aid of a man whose name, strangely enough, was also Edwards forming a rival union. This man managed to form a 'Fifth Column' within both Arch's union and that of George's. By this means he gained access to their balance sheets. These were manipulated and printed with thousands of other leaflets which conveyed the impression that Joseph Arch and George Edwards were using the workers' money for their own ends. This was a complete travesty of the truth. George had long since sacrificed eight shillings per week from his salary as union organiser. Nevertheless, this latest move on behalf of the employers had its effect upon the workers. The rot set in. The end of the unions appeared to be only a matter of time. Even these signs did not cause George to give up the attempt to avert the union's fall. He walked miles addressing numerous mass meetings long distances from his home. He would arrive home very late at night, but would not retire to bed until the early hours of the morning when he had finished writing articles to the press. In these articles he tried to warn the workers of the consequences of forsaking those who had proved to be their true and faithful leaders for those of the rival Edwards's union. He advised those who found themselves denied work not to starve but to put themselves upon the poor law and the rates. In this way he said they could compel the authorities to take notice of their plight.

In a last effort to rally the workers, George persuaded Joseph Arch, now an old man, to visit Cromer to address a mass meeting. The meeting was presided over by Mr Ketton, George's late employer. A real welcome awaited Joseph on his arrival at Cromer. George had arranged for the Cromer and Southrepps brass bands to play him from the house in which he was staying to the lecture hall where the meeting was held. It proved to be a good meeting, but the damage by the fifth columnists of the rival union had been too great for either George or Joseph to repair so that no definite form of unity could be regained at the meeting to ensure the future of the unions.

Alone after the meeting, Joseph Arch, with tears in his eyes said to George:

> My boy, you are younger than I, therefore you will be able to return to work. But take my advice, when you do, never trust our class again. I am getting old, I have given all the best years of my life in their interests and now, in my old age, they have forsaken me.

The workers' apathy and their continued drift from the unions caused George to feel that Arch's advice was sound and his words true. He had himself already made great sacrifice on their behalf. He made yet another by giving up the whole of his salary in order to further ease the situation, all to no apparent avail. The workers continued to refuse to heed his advice. To add further hindrance to his efforts, the weekly paper, *The Eastern Weekly Leader*, in which he had been able to write his articles to draw the public attention to the workers' plight, was compelled to close. This was due to the withdrawal of trading advertisements by way of boycott by the friends of the farming community.

George's final article to this paper was in the form of a warning to the workers. He called them to task for their folly. Having given an outline of his work in connection with the unions, he wrote:

> One thing I can honestly say, in advocating the rights on the working man I have never studied my own personal interests or comfort ... But none of these things have moved me as I felt I was fighting a noble and just cause. But, alas, you, the working men, soon grew 'weary in well-doing,' you allowed a spirit of apathy, of mistrust and wicked prejudice to grow up amongst you. You have believed the vilest calumnies that have been uttered against the leaders of the movement ... hence your failure to emancipate yourselves ... In taking my final farewell of you, let it never be said that George Edwards has left you. It is you that have left him ... I have as strong a faith as ever in the justness of your cause and the justness of your claims to live by labour, but I have lost all faith that you will ever manifest manliness and independence enough to claim your right ... I will say to you, as did Ernest Jones in one of his beautiful poems, because, although you cannot realise it, your cause will one day triumph. Fellow workers, farewell! It is not for me to get the work accomplished, I would have helped you 'But ye would not'. I will say to you:
>
> > Sharpen the sickle; how full the ears!
> > Our children are crying for bread,
> > And the field has been watered with orphans' tears
> > And enriched with their father's dead.

43

> And hopes that are buried, and hearts that broke,
> Lie deep in the treasuring sod:
> Then sweep down the grain with a thunder-stroke,
> In the name of humanity's God'[1]

When he wrote this article, George felt convinced that it really was his final farewell as leader of the land workers. This feeling was further emphasised for him by his defeat in the next district council election. Was it not enough to break the stoutest heart?

Notes

1. Edwards, *Crow Scaring*, pp.92-3.

Chapter 4

The New Union

A friend who had sympathetically viewed George's efforts on behalf of the agricultural worker and the distress it had landed him in, offered him a few weeks' work at Sheringham. This was in February 1896. He felt glad to accept the offer. It was towards the end of April that his work at Sheringham finished and he then accepted an invitation to undertake a speaking tour in Wiltshire by the Land Restoration League. His work for the land workers with its resulting hardships had become known far beyond the borders of his native county.

Whilst this campaign of the league could not be said to have met with much success, it did prove to be a further training ground for George. Incidentally, it prevented him from losing altogether his hope for the future. It also kept him within the sphere of public work on behalf of the poor which, as has been seen, he was very tempted to give up. He returned home the following October quite determined to settle down to a more peaceful life and work upon the land. However, he allowed himself to be nominated once more for the Erpingham Rural District Council and he was returned unopposed. Charlotte was also elected. The next five years saw them both continuing quietly and contentedly their efforts for the poor of the district without experiencing a repetition of the upheavals of the past.

In 1903 the Liberal Party approached George and offered him a position as speaker in their campaign for free trade. This he decided to accept. It necessitated his going away from home to address by-election meetings in different parts of the country. He only returned home once a fortnight to fulfil his duties as a rural district councillor. He continued in this campaign work for three years until 1906. An amusing incident occurred during this campaign. George found himself constantly being interrupted during his speech at one of the meetings by a man who kept shouting, 'You wouldn't do it if you weren't paid for it!' One of the local people who knew the man passed a note to George telling him that this man was living with two women. When next the man interrupted in the same way as before, George quickly responded with the words, 'Yes, and if I were, I couldn't afford to keep two wives.' This amused his audience who shouted with glee, 'That is what he is doing.' Needless to say, the man beat a hasty retreat.

A general election was held in that year, the result of which was a severe defeat for the Tories. It also brought to a close the Liberal free trade campaign and they had no further employment to offer George. He was thus compelled to yet again seek work on the land and this time he hoped he would be able to settle down to a more normal life with his wife Charlotte, and to continue to do what he could for the poor on the local councils.

However, following the defeat of the Tories at the general election, the farmers began another ruthless campaign of dismissal and victimisation against those suspected of having supported the Liberal Party. To George's amazement and disgust the Liberal Party, who had so recently employed him, now appeared to turn a blind eye to the suffering of the workers whose very support had helped to assure their victory. The workers soon grew restless under the hardships resulting from unemployment and eviction. Their thoughts began to turn again to the need for a strong union to assist and protect them. The question was who could lead and organise such a union. Most of their former leaders were either dead or retired. Not surprisingly, therefore, they turned to George who they were aware was still active on their behalf upon the local councils. They soon inundated him with letters appealing to him to assist them in forming a union. But he did not at first feel disposed to take on so great a responsibility. The task appeared too great. Neither did there appear to him a way whereby the necessary funds needed for such a venture could be raised. He was certain any union formed must be stronger than those of the past because the employers' opposition could not be expected to be any less ruthless than hitherto.

For some time George continued to turn down the men's appeals. He said if they could find a younger man who was prepared to take the responsibility of leadership in the formation of a new union, he would be willing to give all the help he could, but he felt himself at the age of fifty-six to be beyond the work. Apart from this, George had not yet fully recovered his faith in their sincerity. He was not sure that they had the courage to assert their right, nor that they would be able to maintain their loyalty to a new union in face of bitter opposition any more than had the membership of past unions.

One evening in June 1906, having returned home from work, George found many more letters appealing to him to take the lead in organising the farm workers. He read through them all, pondering deeply upon the suffering which the letters revealed. He turned to Charlotte and said: 'I do wish these poor people could find someone else to lead them. I don't feel equal to the task.' Charlotte replied: 'You must try, there is no one else who will.' George took her in his arms and quietly reminded her of the very lonely life she had already so often been compelled to live whilst he was giving all his time to public work on behalf of the workers. Their sacrifices he reminded her had brought little success, but much suffering. If he consented to take up the reins once more, he said, it in all probability would result in a repetition of their past experiences. Charlotte, looking George straight in the face, replied, 'If you will make the effort, I will make the sacrifice.' These words had the effect of dispelling any further doubts as to what was the right course to pursue. His faith was renewed and he hesitated no more. The old zeal and fire was rekindled.

No further time was lost. George immediately set about the task of arranging a conference of workers. He wrote to various members of parliament who sympathised with the farm workers and sought their support. Amongst these were Mr Richard (later Sir Richard) Winfrey, Mr A.W. Soames, Sir Robert Price and Mr George Nichols. All of them sent donations, some expressed doubts about the success of the venture, but Richard Winfrey and George Nichols not only sent donations, but also consented to speak at the conference George was arranging. Two other prominent Norfolk gentlemen of that period, Lord Kimberley and Herbert Day of Norwich, sent him donations when they heard of his renewed activity.

The final arrangements being completed, George was able to fix the conference for 6 July 1906 at the Angel Hotel, North Walsham. Richard Winfrey and George Nicholls were the principal speakers. At the start of the conference George said it had been called as the result of numerous appeals he had received from all parts of the Eastern Counties to form a union. He said, should they agree to form a union, experience of past rival unions should be borne in mind. They should not allow that experience to be repeated. Success, he told them, could only result if they resolved to form one united union. Their object should be the securing for the land workers of better conditions, assisting them to obtain allotments and small holdings, the securing of better representation on local authorities and in Parliament. In his opinion union funds should be used for these purposes.

George then went on to warn the conference that they must not think a land workers' union could immediately be formed on the same lines as those unions in the industrial areas. He said the smallness of the land workers' weekly wage prevented that. The great distances to be travelled in organising the workers meant it would be several years before substantial funds could be built up. He ended:

> In my judgement it will take years to build up a union that will be
> effective in altering the conditions of the labourer, but I have faith that it
> can be done, and in due course the labourer will be able to take his place
> with his fellows in the towns. One thing, however, is certain a great deal
> of hard work will have to be done by someone, great sacrifices will have
> to be made, and those responsible for the running of the union will come
> in for a great deal of abuse.

He was destined before long to learn how prophetic his words had been.

Following the principal speaker's address and the discussion, the conference unanimously agreed to the following resolution: 'That this conference of agricultural labourers considers the time has come when steps should be taken to form a union for the agricultural labourers, and that a provisional committee should be formed to carry this into effect.' It was further agreed that the union should be named 'The Eastern Counties Agricultural Labourers' and Small Holders' Union'. Those elected were to form the provisional committee to act to the end of the year and to draw up the union's constitution and rules were: president: George Nicholls, MP; vice-president: W.B. Harris (of Lincolnshire); treasurer: Richard Winfrey, MP (Peterborough); with seven others among whom was Mr Herbert Day of Norwich. George, elected general secretary, had the full weight of the responsibility for organising upon his shoulders. He not only began this task with bearing the physical burden it entailed but also at a financial loss. He had received ten pounds in donations at the conference, but the total expenses came to eleven pounds, so he was one pound out of pocket. Also it had been agreed that he should receive no salary for the first twelve months of the union. He had thus to do some harvest work when he could. But his financial burden was somewhat eased through the kindness of Mr Herbert Day who insisted upon paying him thirteen shillings per week for this first twelve months. It was upon this sum that George, Charlotte and their niece, Blanche Corke, had to live. Blanche was given permission to assist George with the books whilst he was away organising.

George had by this time learnt to ride a cycle which he had acquired. This eased his travelling as hitherto he had to walk miles in meeting the workers. He spent long hours away from home, but Charlotte bravely made her sacrifice and kept the home bright and cheerful for his return. When he held meetings nearer home, however, she would accompany him and help him. She also continued with him upon the local councils. Sunday, which was a day of rest from organising work, was not really a rest day for George. He would then be off on his cycle to conduct services in various primitive methodist chapels in the district. Never once did he allow his union work to become an excuse to neglect his call to preach the gospel.

At the end of the year the provisional committee called a general meeting of the union's membership. It had, in its anxiety to keep all expenditure down to the lowest in the union's early months, appeared to act against its principles of opposition to 'sweated labour' in its attitude to its secretary, George. The matter was fully discussed at the general meeting, and after every item of expenditure was thoroughly scrutinised, their unwillingness to ease George's financial burden and that of general organising work was reversed by the general meeting finally agreeing to grant him twenty-three shillings per week plus travelling and out-of-pocket expenses. They agreed also that his niece should be paid seven shillings per week for book-keeping and that an assistant secretary be appointed at the salary of twenty-five shillings per week. They decided to engage a solicitor to deal with all legal matters.

The rapid growth of the union was the result of the excessively hard work by George. But the strain began to tell on him and his health broke down. He was forced to take a complete rest for three weeks. He steadfastly refused to take any longer, and was soon cycling hundreds of miles rallying the workers into the union ranks. The spirit that kept him going is aptly shown in one of the verses of the songs with which he usually opened his meetings. It was sung to the tune *Sandon* (usually sung to the hymn 'Lead Kindly Light').

> Strong Human love! within whose steadfast will
> Is always peace.
> O stay with me, storm-tossed on waves of ill;
> Let passions cease.
> Come thou in power within my heart to reign,
> For I am weak and struggle has begun.

The resurrection of the land workers union of Norfolk in 1906 coincided with a vacancy occurring in the county council division of Buxton. This was due to the death of Mr Charles Louis Buxton. George was persuaded to accept the invitation to be nominated as the union candidate. Although this caused some anxiety in the Tory camp, the other candidate withdrew and George was elected unopposed. This resulted in the immediate preparation by the local Tories to obtain his defeat at the next county council election. In these efforts they were successful; George was defeated by fifty votes.

However, before long he was given another opportunity to seek re-election by another vacancy arising through the death of the councillor for the Walsingham division. Once more he was nominated by the union members and decided to stand as a Labour candidate. He was disgusted and dismayed to find that the local Liberals supported his Tory opponent, a Mr Walker. This, undoubtedly, prompted his choice of a watchword 'Be just and fear not,' which he had printed on all his bills announcing his meetings. The fight was a very strenuous one. George received little help. He organised the campaign himself, but was fortunate in having the help of two of his union colleagues, the assistant secretary, Mr Thacker and Mr Green. Between them they did all the clerical work and addressed meetings in every parish of the constituency. The campaign lasted for three weeks, the workers rallied to the poll in large numbers, although many of them had to walk three or four miles to get there after a hard day's work. The count proved very exciting; it was taken in the returning officer's house. Upon arrival there George and his agent found to their surprise that his opponent's agent was the returning officer's son, and had in fact been acting as deputy-returning officer. A strong protest against this was made.

At the close of the count the returning officer declared that both candidates had polled an equal number of votes. George was not satisfied, because the number of votes was found not to correspond to that of the counterfoils. He demanded a recount, following which the result still remained the same, but four papers were found missing. It was then that George's colleague detected four papers under the mirror. These were found to be George's votes. Of course, no one professed to knowing how they got under the mirror, but they were valid and George was duly declared elected. He was the first direct Labour representative to be elected to the Norfolk County Council. He very soon became elected to those committees in which his chief interests were. Amongst these were smallholdings, public health and old age pensions.

A further honour came to George in September 1907 when the union appointed him their representative to the Trades Union Congress which was held at Ipswich. When he rose to put the land workers view upon the troublesome question of the tied cottage, he was given a great reception. He forcefully presented a sound case for the abolition of tied cottages. He read a copy of an agreement which so many land workers were compelled to sign before the farmer would employ them or allow them to live in his cottage. It was as follows:

> I the undersigned agree to hire the cottage in the parish of ... the property of ... at a rental of ... and agree to give the cottage up at a week's notice should the landlord require it for any other workman. I also agree not to keep any pigs or fowls without first obtaining permission from the landlord or his agent. I will also act as night-watchman when required, and give any information I may have that will lead to the conviction of anyone seen poaching on the estate. I also undertake not to harbour any of my family who may misconduct themselves in any way. I also agree on leaving my cottage to hand over my copper and oven to the landlord or his agent and not to disturb the bricks or remove these utensils until the landlord or his agent have refused to purchase them. I will also undertake to live at peace with my neighbours and to lead an honest and respectable life. I will, before admitting any of my family home, apply to the landlord or his agent for permission, giving particulars on a form provided by the landlord, their names and ages, also if married or single, and how long they want to stay.[1]

This agreement George told congress, made the workers virtually slaves to the will of their employers.

The production of this agreement so impressed the congress that they passed unanimously a resolution urging Labour members of parliament to take up the question forthwith. As a result of George's efforts at the congress the question of the tied cottage was brought before the public eye. He found himself inundated with letters from all parts of the country requesting further information upon the treatment of the land workers. This gave the union greater impetus for its task, and its membership continued to increase, a very encouraging sign to George that his efforts were at last bearing fruit. But as regards the vexed question of the tied cottage he found he had to continue the fight for its abolition until his dying day. Indeed it was not until the Agricultural Act of 1976 that the tied cottage in the form he knew it was abolished, forty-three years after George's death.

Before contesting the Walsingham by-election, George had promised the workers of Freebridge, King's Lynn, that he would be their candidate at the next county council election. This promise he fulfilled in 1910. His colleague, Robert Green, took his place in the Walsingham contest. As a result George had very little help in his fight, but amongst those who did help at his meetings were Mr Tom Higdon, a school teacher at Burston, near Diss, who had recently begun to take an active interest in politics and the union for which he and his wife had to pay the price a few years later. Also Mr James Coe of Castleacre (later also becoming union organiser, county councillor and county alderman) loyally supported George in this campaign. Although the opposition proved very strong, since his Tory opponent had the help of many Tory councillors who had themselves been returned unopposed, the union members rallied to the poll and George was elected by a majority of eighty.

This was the final election for the county council he had to fight, and he was re-elected to the committees on which he had previously served. A new attitude now prevailed towards him. Hitherto he had felt he was looked upon with suspicion, rather as something of below average intelligence by other members of the Council. But now he found all treated him with the greatest respect and listened to him with deepest interest.

George's enthusiasm and inexperience when first elected to the county council had caused him to believe that smallholdings could easily be obtained for the land workers, and that better treatment for the aged and improved health services would be conceded. But by the time of his final election, experience had taught him otherwise. He soon had to realise that he was up against a great problem and very stiff opposition. The act relating to the granting of smallholdings by county councils was, George found, so bound up by red tape which safeguarded the landlord's interest that councils had great difficulty in obtaining the necessary land which could be let at a rent the workers could afford to pay. As a consequence, only a fraction of the hundreds of applicants for smallholdings were successful. Although unsuccessful in obtaining the relief he desired for the land workers with regard to smallholdings, he was successful in another sphere of his county council work that of the mentally sick in the mental hospitals. He was able to obtain certain beneficial dietary changes and some improvement in the social life of these unfortunate people. His interest in this work continued to the end of his days.

Notes

1.   Edwards, *Crow Scaring*, p. 126.

Chapter 5

Crisis

The period of his county council campaign and activities was a strenuous one for George, for he did not relax in any way his efforts on behalf of his union. He cycled hundreds of miles throughout Norfolk in addition to those in connection with his county council elections. As he travelled through the villages and towns he came very much aware of the approach of yet another crisis in agriculture. The men were becoming dissatisfied and restless. They openly declared that they thought it was about time more direct action was taken towards obtaining what they felt they deserved by way of increased wages and better conditions.

George, in conveying these sentiments to the union's executive, tried to impress upon them the danger prevalent in the position, but he had little success. Their desire to keep expenditure within the narrowest limits blinded them to the signs and deafened them to George's warnings. A resolution was passed at the annual general meeting at King's Lynn on 19 March 1910, calling upon the executive to take steps to secure at once the saturday half-day, a shorter working day all the year round and one shilling per week wage increase. Even this did not rouse the executive to the real position. They steadfastly refused to grant George any additional help or allow him to call them together in face of any emergency that might arise. It was said he was quite capable of handling the situation himself. He left this meeting heavy-hearted and filled with many grave forebodings. He was of the opinion that the executive was letting the men down and that they were placing too big a responsibility upon his shoulders. But despite his forebodings he began at once to prepare for the crisis, the coming of which he had not long to wait.

On 5 April 1910 he received a letter from the secretary of the Trunch union branch informing him that its members had objected to working ten hours per day without receiving a shilling per week increase. George wrote back at once requesting the secretary to call a special meeting of its members on 11 April so that he could meet and discuss with them the best method to adopt. Meanwhile he advised them to take no action. However, before the meeting could take place the farmers had given their men notice terminating their employment. George was most anxious to prevent a prolonged and bitter struggle. He lost no time in contacting the secretary of the Farmers'

Federation, whom he asked to persuade his members not to import labour. At the same time George undertook to endeavour to get the men to agree to work until the representatives of both sides could meet to discuss the situation. The Federation secretary agreed to this and in addition promised to try to get the farmers to reinstate all the men without prejudice to pending negotiations.

George, with Herbert Day, Robert Green and Mr Codling of the executive, put the Farmers' Federation secretary's reply before the Trunch members. It was decided to act upon their advice and return to work. Then George straightaway wrote to the federation secretary and informed him that the men had agreed to a truce. In view of this, he told the federation secretary the opportunity should be taken by the federation to meet the workers' representatives and form a joint committee to try, by discussion, to settle the whole question of hours and wages. Only then, George said, could the interests of both sides be assured and avoid a recurrence of any unpleasantness in the future. Unfortunately, he received no reply to this letter. He was thus not surprised to hear within the next few days that the farmers had broken the truce and were demanding the men to work a ten-hour day. This the men resolutely refused to do. All hope of a settlement was destroyed. George was requested to urge his executive to support them. When they met the executive agreed to do so.

At the start of the dispute the farmers did all they could to provoke the men. They imported labour whom they paid ten shillings per week more than they had paid their own men. But George's leadership kept members of the union steadfast and calm in face of this provocation. During this dispute a strange thing happened. One of the farms where some of the locked-out men had worked came up for sale. On George's advice, as many men as could do so applied to the county council for smallholdings. He used his influence on the Smallholdings Committee to get the council to purchase the farm. The result was that some of the men eventually became tenants of the very farm where they had been refused work. The consequences of these efforts was that he earned the animosity of many farmers and landlords. So great was this in some quarters that the men feared for his safety when he cycled to and from union meetings. They formed a bodyguard and escorted him safely in and out of the villages whilst the dispute continued.

The Trunch strike dragged on for six months, but was eventually settled to the men's satisfaction. However, the soundness of George's warnings to his executive was soon further emphasised when trouble broke out at St Faith's near Norwich. Here matters quickly came to a head in May. The branch secretary urged George to meet the members and discuss the question of hours and wages so that a right way of meeting their demands could be found. George had been instructed not to call a full executive meeting of the union when a dispute arose, but only those executive members living nearest to the area of the dispute. In the case of the St Faith's crisis George, following this ruling, called Herbert Day, Robert Green and Thomas Thacker to meet with him and the St Faith's members on 14 May. Every member of the branch attended; their secretary, George Hewitt (who later became a leading member of the National Union of Agricultural Workers), presided. The men stated that they desired a shilling per week increase to bring their wages to fourteen shillings. They also wanted to finish work at one o'clock on Saturdays. They said their employers had adopted a very unreasonable attitude to their request and as a result their patience with the employers had reached breaking point. They felt they should now hand in their notices.

George realised that a great deal of tact was called for to prevent a most serious situation from arising. He appealed to them to try all peaceful means first before resorting to a strike. If they failed and were compelled to strike he personally would support them whatever the consequences might be for him. They agreed to take his advice and await the reply to a letter he offered to write on their behalf to every employer in the district. In this letter George asked the employers if they would agree to grant a shilling per week increase and to arrange the men's working hours so that they could finish work at one o'clock on Saturdays. He arranged the next meeting with the St Faith's branch for 20 May to hear the farmers' reply. The letter that George wrote showed that, should a strike become inevitable, neither he nor the men could be blamed for not having endeavoured to resolve their problems by negotiation first. He ended his letter by saying:

> We would be glad to meet a number of the employers and discuss this matter and come to some reasonable arrangement and thus prevent any dispute arising between you and your men with all the suffering and inconvenience that must inevitably follow.

But his letter was ignored.

The special meeting of the St Faith's branch was attended in full strength, but Herbert Day was the only executive member who was present with George. The failure of the farmers to reply to George's letter made the men angry. They interpreted this as a sign that their employers were unwilling either to discuss or to accede to their request for an increase in wages and amendment of working hours. They unanimously requested

George and Herbert Day to grant them permission to strike. Although George believed that the union executive was wrong to have placed so great a responsibility upon so few of its members, and as there now appeared no alternative to strike action, he and Herbert Day agreed to the men's wishes. Thus began another long and protracted dispute. As at Trunch, so at St Faith's. The farmers used every means they could to provoke the men, refusing again and again George's several appeals to them to meet the workers' representatives.

To gain support and financial help for those on strike, George cycled miles organising demonstrations. In this he was greatly helped by various Norwich Labour and trade union leaders, in particular Walter Smith and William Holmes, both of whom later became leaders of the National Union of Agricultural Workers and played a prominent part in the Labour movement.[1] Collections were taken at various factory gates in Norwich. Mr Winfrey was able to offer work to several men upon his farm at Walpole, near King's Lynn.

Although each day brought George fresh abuse from his opponents who accused him of feathering his own nest and of setting employees against employers, he was not so much affected by that as by the attitude of some members of the union's executive who, in their desire to save the union's funds, appeared prepared to end the strike upon terms dictated by the employers. On 30 July 1910, the executive held its first meeting since the outbreak of the two strikes. It was held in the union's new headquarters at Wensum House, Hempton, Fakenham. A report was received of a letter received by Mr Arnett (an executive member) from a Mr Leadbeater, a schoolmaster at St Faith's who offered to negotiate with the employers with a view to taking the men back at thirteen shillings per week, the wage which had caused the strike. George most strongly protested against this, but he was overruled. It was decided that each branch secretary in the area of the St Faith's dispute should be circularised. They were to be asked to call special meetings of their members to decide whether the six months' strike should be brought to an honourable end by their executive. They were told that it had cost the union £900. The secretaries were asked to put the numbers for and against on a ballot paper provided and return the same immediately to George. To George's amazement the executive inserted nothing in the circular about the terms on which the executive committee would seek to bring about 'an honourable conclusion' of the strike.

The result of the ballot showed a majority of 756 for ending the strike. George was instructed to contact Mr Arnett and direct him to write to

Leadbeater. Leadbeater was authorised to meet the farmers on behalf of the union. When the farmers' reply was received it was to the effect that they would not consent to take all the men back, and in any case only a few at a time as their imported labour became disposed of. George immediately summoned the executive to meet on 17 December. When the employers' terms were read out it caused a most heated debate. Mr Day and George strongly opposing the acceptance of them. They moved a resolution that Mr Leadbeater be thanked for his efforts, but, in view of the unsatisfactory terms offered by the farmers, present negotiations should be brought to an end. An equal number voted for and against this resolution, but the chairman's casting vote carried it.

A further resolution was similarly passed calling for another ballot to be taken asking the men whether or not the strike should continue for fourteen shillings with the added guarantee that all men would be taken back at once. The preparation of these ballot papers entailed much work for George. It meant that in order to get them completed and dispatched he had to work through the night. But his efforts proved in vain. Before the ballot could be counted certain executive members demanded another meeting which, although hotly contested by George, Herbert Day and Mr Codling, overruled the previous meeting decision. Mr Nicholls, the president, and Mr Winfrey, the treasurer, were appointed to negotiate with the farmers with a view to ending the strike. It was ended upon the old basis of thirteen shillings per week. Only thirty-three out of the seventy-five men were taken back, the remainder the union had to support. The irony of it was that when the ballot was counted it showed a majority of forty-nine in favour of continuing the strike.

The strike at Trunch had ended successfully for the men. The union had made progress as a result. The dispute at St Faith's, lasting eight months, ended, not by the will of the men, nor through exhaustion of union funds, but because the majority of the union executive believed it was in the men's best interest. The final outcome seemed likely to be the complete break-up of the union to which George had devoted the best years of his life. He became weighed down with anxiety, believing his life's work was swiftly drawing to its close.

The union held its annual general meeting in the Fakenham Assembly Rooms (part of the old Corn Hall, which became first the Central Cinema and is now a bingo hall), on 25 February 1911. It proved to be a very stormy meeting. Practically every branch of the union was represented. The executive in addition to having ended the St Faith's strike, had also refused their union branch's request for a special meeting on 12 January to consider the question. Their action was hotly contested and severely condemned. Some members of the executive, in defending their action, bitterly attacked George and Herbert Day for having supported the strike action. The tone of the meeting seemed to emphasise and highlight deep division in the union ranks, and George feared that the only possible outcome would surely be the complete break-up of the union. However, this time his fears did not materialise, although the president and treasurer (George Nicholls and Richard Winfrey) resigned and immediately left the meeting. Walter Smith and Herbert Day were elected in their place. George Hewitt, of St Faith's, William Holmes and James Coe were among the new executive selected to support them.

The first job the new executive tackled was the easing of the suffering of the victims of the two strikes and helping George in the complete reorganisation of the union. The result of this was that the burden and worry he had hitherto been compelled to shoulder himself became considerably eased. Through their united effort George was able to report by the time of the next annual meeting the enroling of 617 new members and the formation of twenty-one new branches. Also he was able to report the re-starting of several branches that had become defunct. His report showed that the progress made had been accomplished by the co-operation he had from James Coe and Mr Codling. Coe, attending meetings in Norfolk, Oxfordshire and Kent, cycled 3,240 miles: Codling attended 242 meetings, walked 202 miles and cycled 2,840 miles; George had attended 183 meetings in Norfolk, Oxfordshire and Kent. Apart from this, he had attended eighty-three rural district council meetings, cycling 1,866 miles. He also travelled 1,563 miles by train. During the same period he had represented the union at the Trades Union Congress in Newcastle, where he had been elected a member of a delegation to the President of the Board of Trade on behalf of the agricultural workers. The union annual meeting showed their continued confidence in their new executive and George, their general secretary, by re-electing them en bloc for the ensuing year. They also appointed a Mr Robert Walker to be full-time assistant general secretary, Miss Pike resigned as the work was becoming too much for her.

It was at the height of his joy in the resurrection of the union, and his renewed battles against the bitter opposition of the employers, that he suffered a blow of a different nature, the repercussions of which he felt for a long time. It was one which took all his strength and will-power to combat in order to keep going. Charlotte's health became cause for anxiety and it was found that she was suffering from cancer and was soon confined to her bed. George never left her side as her condition became increasingly worse. She died on 24 April 1912, two days after her seventieth birthday. Elizabeth Kernick, George's niece, a trained nurse, had lovingly cared for her aunt and nursed her during her last days. Upon Charlotte's death, Elizabeth felt very deeply for her uncle's distress and consented to bring her family to live with him in order to look after him. She had herself recently lost her husband. In this way she not only was herself able to have a fresh interest in life to take her mind off her own sad experience, but also at the same time to considerably ease her uncle's burden.

At this time trouble was brewing on the Lancashire farms which resulted in a strike of two thousand men. They had demanded the right to cease work at one o'clock on Saturdays with a minimum wage of twenty-four shillings per week with sixpence per hour overtime, plus recognition of the union. Despite the physical conditions resulting from his bereavement, George insisted that he could not rest, but must do all he could to assist the Lancashire farm workers. He, with Walter Smith, failed to get a settlement without recourse to strike action. However, the men's determination eventually led to the granting of a rise of two shillings per week, sixpence per hour overtime and were allowed to finish work at 3 pm on Saturdays. This was the first time in their history that the farm worker had obtained a reduction in hours of labour.

Upon his return home George collapsed, suffering from the reaction of this campaign and the severe strain of his bereavement. He was compelled to take a complete rest. At the end of a month he was still unable to carry on his work. In view of the greatly increased union membership, and the fact that the union had now become an approved society, further complicating the general secretary's work, George concluded he must give the job up. His executive reluctantly accepted his resignation and Robert Walker, the assistant secretary, was appointed in his place. But they insisted that George should be given a free hand to do whatever organising work he still felt able to do.

These experiences caused George again to assume that his life's work was drawing rapidly to its close. It was with these thoughts in mind whilst sitting quietly at home under the loving care of his niece, Elizabeth, that he penned what he believed to be his final farewell to his fellow workers and the union. In it he said, due to his age and indifferent health, he felt the time had come for him to lay down the responsibilities of the union. It was published in the local press under the heading:

George Edwards
Farewell Message to Norfolk Labourers
Hands Over the Reins to Younger Men

The strain of the recent strike in Lancashire has completely broken me down ... The loss of my dear wife twelve months since was the first blow from which I have never recovered ... I have lived to see one victory gained for shorter hours and increases in wages. I had hoped to be able to have kept in harness until greater improvements were made in the life of my Norfolk brethren. But the wheels of progress move too slowly, and age, with all the infirmities stops for nothing. I must now leave the work for younger men to take up and carry forward to a successful issue. I have the greatest faith that the work will continue. The union has come to stay .... The hand that has grasped this great social plough and all the poisonous social seeds have been turned up and destroyed.

He then urged the men to be loyal to their union and its leaders for upon their action ended the future of their movement. He ended his farewell message with the words:

May the God of heaven help you in your work of human love and human emancipation. I would have gone further but my labour is over.

But take courage then, my brother!
The day will come at last,
The clouds are lifting quickly,
The night is breaking fast.
Be strong, then, of good courage,
Our cause is just and right,
And he who holds by justice
Is sure to win the fight.[2]

Notes

1. Walter Smith, one-time President of the Union, became MP for Norwich, a representative of the Boot and Shoe trade union. William Holmes was President and later General Secretary of the NUAW in the 1930s.

2. *Eastern Weekly Press*, 26 July 1913.

Chapter 6

The War Years, 1914-1918

Elizabeth Kernick, his niece, continued to care for George. It was due to her expert nursing that he was able gradually to recover from his illness. The wound of his loss of Charlotte slowly healed and he began to take a new interest in life. As his strength returned so did the desire within him awaken to take an active part once more in the improvement of the lot of his fellows. His faith became renewed.

4. *Elizabeth Kernick, Sir George's niece and housekeeper (1912-23), and the author's mother.*

The first thing he inquired for when he was able to get about again was his bicycle. But the doctor had warned him that to attempt cycling again would result in overtaxing his heart. Elizabeth had foreseen this possibility and before he had fully recovered and was still confined to bed, she asked if she could sell his cycle as the doctor had advised against his riding again. George, feeling rather low at that moment, had agreed and Elizabeth took him at his word. However, when he was on his feet again he somewhat regretted his hasty decision, particularly when he realised that his travelling would be much restricted. It meant that he would have to rely solely upon the local rail services which were very limited. But this was really a blessing for him because it was an easier mode of travelling and gave him a chance to fully recover without set-back through straining his heart again by the effort of cycling.

In 1914 George was appointed a county justice of the peace. But it was really two major issues which accentuated his return to the limelight of public work in 1914. One, chiefly affecting the county of Norfolk, was the Burston School Strike. The other was the outbreak of World War I. First, the Burston School Strike. Burston, a little village near Diss, had for its schoolmaster and mistress, Mr and Mrs Tom Higdon. They were two kind-hearted people who were much devoted to their profession and the children they taught. Both children and parents loved and respected them. Unfortunately for the Higdons they were of a different school of thought religiously and politically to that of their school managers who were two Church of England clergymen and their wives.

The spark that finally caused the trouble appeared to be that Tom Higdon had allied himself to George's Agricultural Workers' Union. He had become one of its most ardent workers in his spare time. He had been speaking at numerous meetings. Charges, accusing them of cruelty to a group of children at the school, were brought against him and his wife which resulted in an inquiry on 23 and 29 February 1914. The outcome was that the charges were proved to be of a trifling nature which should never have been made or brought against them. Yet, in spite of this, they were both dismissed on 31 March. The parents of the children immediately reacted by withdrawing their children from the school. They refused to allow them to be taught by any other teacher whom the education committee sent. They were summoned to appear at the magistrates court and were convicted and fined. A huge demonstration was held on Burston Common which was attended by two thousand people. They demanded a public inquiry into the dismissal of the Higdons. George was one of the principal speakers. He was convinced that the dismissal was a clear-cut case of victimisation. He conducted the demonstration upon religious lines, basing his address upon the text, 'Thou shalt not bear false witness against thy neighbour.'

However, George was not content to merely address demonstrations on behalf of his friends the Higdons, but together with his union colleagues, Herbert Day, W.B. Taylor and James Coe, he championed their cause on the Norfolk County Council. There they demanded, in the interest of peace and well-being of the children, that an effort be made to bring the Burston trouble to an end in a way that would be satisfactory to all parties concerned. In addressing the council George said,

> I have long since learned that there are two sides to every question. Therefore to secure peace there must be a little give and take by both parties concerned. I would like, therefore, to pathetically appeal to you, in the interests of peace, to carefully consider if you could re-instate Mr and Mrs Higdon to their former positions, and they on their part undertaking to work quietly and to have no public demonstration, which I believe they are willing to do.

George added a warning that unless something was done in the direction of peace the whole trade union movement would take the matter up.

This advice was refused. The trade union movement took the matter up throughout the country. Public sympathy was roused on behalf of the Higdons, hundreds of pounds were subscribed and a new school was built. It was called the Burston Strike School and the Higdons became the teachers in it. It was indeed a monument to a great fight for political and religious freedom. It still stands today as a monument to that fight. George said in later years when looking back to these events, 'I have never regretted the part I took in this great fight. I am, however, satisfied that had the county council taken my advice at the time, most of this unpleasantness might have been avoided.'[1]

With the outbreak of World War I George saw the liberty of the poor again threatened. At that time he could not see any alternative to war which his country could adopt to meet this new threat to its liberty and life. He believed it to be his duty to put all personal considerations aside. He himself was too old to enlist for military service. He decided he could best serve his country by assisting in the recruiting campaign. So during the early stages of the war he was in this way instrumental in inducing several young people to enlist. This caused alarm among his many pacifist colleagues within the labour movement. They feared he was carrying his patriotism too far. But being convinced he was doing right, he followed the dictates of his conscience. It was when the war continued to drag on with increasing ferocity and bitterness that he began to doubt the rightness of his attitude.

With the passing of the Military Service Act he and George Hewitt were appointed to serve as their union representatives upon the Appeal Tribunal. In this role they were able to look after the interests of the land workers. Often George found the task unpleasant when he was called upon to judge people he knew to be sincere conscientious objectors to military service, as is shown by the following reply he wrote to one such objector who had requested him to write a letter to the Appeal Tribunal to testify his sincerity:

7 Lichfield Street
Queens Road
Fakenham
4/7/16
Dear Mr Housdon,

Sorry there has been delay in answering your letter. But I have been from home all the week. You are quite right in saying that I have known you to be a conscientious objector to all kind of war for many years. But to write you a letter to be presented to the Appeal Tribunal as a member of an appeal tribunal such tribunals being appointed by the Crown I am afraid it would be an illegal act. But however, much I may think the attitude of objectors is illogical I think all who are sincere in their belief ought to have the benefit of the Act.

Yours faithfully,
Geo. Edwards

As time went along, doubts began to form in his own mind that his own attitude had been at fault. Particularly so as the horror of war had increased, and he felt the rightness of the stand of many of his sincere objector friends was being emphasised by the result of the war on combatants and non-combatants alike. This led him to express himself thus:

I would never undertake it again should the occasion arise, which I hope never will ... I am bitterly disappointed at the result of the war. It (the war) has entirely changed my outlook on war and its causes, that force is no remedy, and that unless the nations disarm and men devote their great inventive and scientific powers in the direction of peace, civilised man will soon be utterly destroyed.[2]

Prophetic words, which despite the world's experience of a Second World War since George's death, could still be echoed and the warning still needs heeding.

In addition to his other war-time activities, George and his colleague, George Hewitt, served upon the Norfolk War Agricultural Executive Committee as workers' representatives. They were instrumental there in helping ex-servicemen who were unfit for further military service. They were also able to help in assuring that the maximum amount of arable land was brought back into cultivation to ensure maintenance of food supplies. George also served upon the Food Control and War Pensions Committees.

The outbreak of war had resulted in the rise in the cost of living, and as the war dragged on so the cost of living continued to rise. But the wages of the land worker did not correspondingly rise. This caused much dissatisfaction amongst them. They informed the Union that if something was not done about it they would consider taking matters into their own hands. The union appealed to the farmers to meet them at a conference to discuss the matter, but they refused. As no action had been taken by the spring of 1915 by the farmers to meet the men's demands, the Union had no alternative but to issue notices to the farmers that if the existing conditions were not improved for the workers the men would cease work. Attending a County Council meeting the following Saturday, George was approached by two leading Norfolk farmers, Mr Keith of Egmere and Mr Overman of Weasenham. They requested him to meet five other influential farmers with the object of finding an amicable solution to the threatened strike. George told them he had no authority to do such a thing and could not obtain authority owing to the union president, Walter Smith, being away from the city at that time. They pointed out to George that neither they nor those whom they wished him to meet were members of the Farmers' Federation, but they were in a position to bring great pressure to bear upon that organisation. They suggested he should meet them unofficially to consider if it were possible to get an official conference called the following week. To this he agreed upon the condition that Herbert Day, the union's treasurer, was present with him, and that under no circumstance would the meeting be considered or implied to be official. Mr Keith and Mr Overman both agreed to this. Later in the day George and Herbert Day met the farmers. After a lengthy discussion in which the farmers admitted that they thought the Federation had done wrong in refusing to meet the men's representatives, it was agreed that both parties should use their influence to get a conference called and to ensure that any agreement reached there would be adhered to.

When the union executive met there was some criticism of the action George and Herbert Day had taken, but they agreed to meet the farmers. This conference was held in the Crown Hotel at Fakenham. The union president ably and forcefully put the men's case for a five-shilling per week increase to bring their wages up to one pound. After retiring to discuss the matter the farmers returned to suggest an increase of three shillings on condition that the union obtained the withdrawal of the men's notices. George and his colleagues agreed to accept the farmers' offer. In this way he helped to prevent a disastrous strike, whilst at the same time achieving a forty-one year old ambition in the initiation of collective bargaining between workers and farmers.

Due to the continued agitation of the union through their representative in parliament, Noel Buxton (later Lord Noel-Buxton) it was not long before collective bargaining between employers and employees in the agricultural industry became recognised as essential by the government of the day. Early in 1917 Lloyd George brought in a bill called the Corn Production Act which set up an Agricultural Wages Board, and at the same time fixed the minimum wage at twenty-five shillings per week. The union made great endeavours to get this figure in the bill altered to thirty shillings but without success.

The new wages board consisted of sixteen workers' representatives and sixteen employers' representatives with seven independent members. These latter being appointed by the government. It was the independent members who had the responsibility of deciding the issue should the other two parties fail to reach agreement. Eight of the employers' and workers' representatives were appointed by the Ministry of Agriculture (George was appointed in this way). The other sixteen members were appointed by the workers' union and the Farmers' Federation.

The first meeting of the Central Wages Board formed a committee for each county. Each side of the industry were left to select their own representatives. George was elected to the Norfolk committee where he became the leader of the workers' representatives. As such he moved that wages should be raised to thirty shillings for a fifty-four hour week and the working week to end at 1 pm on Saturday. The employers' representatives rejected this by moving an amendment to retain wages at twenty-five shillings and hours as then prevailing. The appointed members adjourned the meeting for two weeks in the hope that by that time agreement would be reached.

At the adjourned meeting the employers offered twenty-seven shillings and sixpence for fifty-seven hours. This George and his colleagues refused.

A compromise by the appointed members of thirty shillings for fifty-five and a half hours was rejected by the farmers but reluctantly agreed to by George and his colleagues. The appointed members gave their vote for it and it was carried. The resolution was then forwarded to the Central Wages Board who rejected it, accepting instead the workers' original claim for thirty shillings for fifty-four hours with working time finishing at one o'clock on Saturdays. All time over these hours was to be paid as overtime at the rate of time and a quarter for six days and time and a half of Sundays. Horsemen and stockmen's wages were also raised in proportion.

Unfortunately the wages board notices announcing these changes were somewhat vaguely worded. The result was that much misunderstanding arose in the interpretation of them. Some believed the new rates were to apply immediately, whilst the farmers generally thought it to be later. George found himself severely criticised because he interpreted the notice as bringing the new wage and hours structure into being one month following the board's meeting. Some of his colleagues inferred that he was taking sides with the farmers. He challenged the accusation and was proved to be right in his interpretation, but not before several disputes had arisen. This caused him much heartache because he knew had they not occurred the men would have benefited earlier than they did. As it was the Board at their next meeting, whilst confirming the Order, postponed it to take effect three months after the end of the war. With the end of the war the men received the increase and the Saturday half-day. George thus saw the fulfilment of yet another ambition for the Norfolk land workers. It was one he had worked to attain for them so long against so many odds.

Early in 1918, as the general election was approaching, George publicly announced his intention to leave the Liberal Party to join the Labour Party which he now was convinced more really stood for the true interests of the working-class of the two parties. The union, following a ballot of its members, had already decided to take political action by becoming affiliated to the Labour Party. The executive decided to place their own candidates in the electoral field. Every branch was requested to forward its nominations. This being done, five names from those nominated were sent out again for the branches to vote upon, the three receiving the highest votes were then accepted as the union's official candidates. George's name was one of the three. Following this he was invited to attend a meeting called to select a prospective Labour candidate for the South Norfolk division. The invitation was accepted and George addressed the meeting upon current affairs, severely criticising the government's war policy. He claimed that the war could have been ended some months before with a saving of many lives had the opportunity been seized of entering into negotiation. He declared that in joining the ranks of the Labour Party he had not given up any principle that he had previously held, but he stood where he had always stood for the raising of the workers' standard of life. After his speech he retired from the room whilst the party delegates considered whether or not he should be their candidate. When he was recalled the chairman, Mr E.G. Gooch, informed him that the delegates had unanimously decided to invite him to become the prospective Labour candidate to contest the division at the forthcoming general election. George thanked them and accepted the invitation.

Quite a hue and cry arose amongst the farming community when it became public knowledge that he had been selected as Labour candidate. As was to be expected, the Liberals made much of his forsaking their cause. He was severely attacked in the press. But George left his answer to his critics to the time of his formal adoption meeting at the start of the election campaign. In this address his clear insight into the future was shown and is worth quoting at length. He began,

> The Government said they wanted a mandate. What greater mandate could they have than a united country to back them up in their peace terms. What was wanted was a just and permanent peace, with no vindictiveness, and the Labour Party held the view that there was no safeguard for a permanent peace except on the grounds laid down by President Wilson. The Labour Party was going in for a League of Nations, for such a league laid down on the president's principles would mean a permanent peace and bring about universal brotherhood. They meant by a League of Nations a league which should consist of all the civilised nations of the world, and that there should be such international dealings with all questions which would prevent war in the future. What I understand when the president talks about a League of Nations and no boycott is that there should be no preferential tariffs, and that all the nations should be dealt with alike. I wish those who talk about boycotting the Germans and taxing their goods out of existence would think for a moment. Germany is too big a nation to be crushed, and the war had taught us that German science and inventions were not dear. If it is attempted to crush her she would prepare for another war, and England and other nations would also have to prepare, and the past war would be nothing as compared to the next ... We in the Labour Party ask for a living wage for all workers, and our class, having made the sacrifice they had, and I am not saying other classes have

not done their bit, are not going back to pre-war conditions. We are advocating a wage in agriculture that will enable parents to raise healthy children. The first function of the party when it comes into power would be to see that this long-neglected class was lifted up above the poverty line on which it has for so long existed. Everything comes from the land and if the farmer was to pay a living wage, agriculture must be so organised that he could do so. The farmer must have security of tenure, this he had not ... There must be security of tenure for the farmers, and although I am a Free Trader, I should be in favour of the clause of the Corn Production Act being strengthened so that the farmer can pay the wage which might be fixed from time to time. But, although I do not expect to see it, I believe the real solution finally rests in land nationalisation. The housing problem was serious. If the Government can find money for war they could find money for houses. Also proper medical attention must be put within the reach of the poorest by the National Insurance Act being radically altered. There must be state-paid medical attendants.

At the end of his speech George received a tremendous ovation. He was forthwith formally adopted. His colleagues of the union and the divisional party immediately began most enthusiastically to work for his election to parliament. Strange are the ways of life that it turned out that George's opponent was the eldest son of the man for whom he had in 1885 worked so hard to get elected as a Liberal. He proved an honourable opponent and did his best personally to see the contest was kept clean. Neither he nor George indulged in personalities. Upon one occasion they even occupied the same pitch at a factory meeting in Wymondham where they each spoke for ten minutes. Mr E.G. Gooch was George's agent. This job he undertook in an honorary capacity. He organised meetings throughout the large constituency. These meetings were crowded with enthusiastic supporters. But the forces of the two, then major parties, Liberal and Tory, were ranged against him. To his amazement and sorrow some leading local methodists joined the forces against him and were vehement in their opposition to him. This combined with the clever propaganda put out by his opponents attacking him for his present war policy. They compared it unfavourably with that of his war-time recruitment activity. It was implied that his present views were hypocritical and his conduct tantamount to treachery. His defeat was thus further ensured. The result of the poll, declared at the Shire Hall, Norwich, was:

Cozens Hardy	11,755
Edwards	6,595
Coalition Majority	5,159

Despite the abuse that George had received from some quarters, he always maintained in later years that this contest had been the cleanest political contest he had ever fought. Nevertheless, the strain upon him was considerable. After writing a letter of thanks to his loyal supporters, he returned to his home at Fakenham, a tired and worn-out man.

Notes

1. The story of Burston is well told in B. Edwards, *The Burston School Strike*, (London, 1974).
2. Edwards, *Crow Scaring*, p. 192.

Chapter 7

OBE, MP

It was during December 1918, whilst he was still suffering from the effects of his recent political battle, and subsequent defeat, that George received news that did much to cheer him and lighten his burden. It came in the formal notice from the Secretary of State that the Prime Minister had been pleased to recommend King George V to appoint him to the rank of Officer in the Civil Division of the Excellent Order of the British Empire. On 3 January, 1919, he was gazetted in the New Year's Honours List as George Edwards, OBE. He received a command from the Lord Chamberlain to appear at Buckingham Palace in February to receive the decoration at the hands of the King.

Returning to his hotel after the ceremony, the strain of the journey and the excitement of the investiture reacted upon his health. Elizabeth, who had accompanied him, tried hard to persuade her uncle to stay in bed at the hotel rather than risk the consequences of further strain by the train journey home. But he was determined to get home despite the risk. However, when he did reach home his health was such that he was compelled to take a complete rest for a month.

During his convalescence a rather amusing incident occurred one morning. The army had commandeered a large house with an adjoining shop opposite to where George lived in Fakenham. Here some of the men were billeted and stored equipment. It was the custom for an officer to drill his men in the street each day right in front of George's front window. This particular morning an officer, a bullying type of man, was shouting and swearing profusely at the men. George heard him threaten to have the men sent overseas. This was too much for him. He then went straight to the officer and confronted him, telling him he had no right to talk to his men in the manner he was, and no right to threaten them with overseas service. The officer pulled himself up to his full height and said: 'Do you know to whom you're talking? I'll have you arrested for interfering with His Majesty's officer whilst he's carrying out his duty. George replied: 'I know very well who you are, but do *you know* to whom you're talking?' Whilst he was addressing the officer he pinned the OBE medal on his lapel and continued,

'Now, rather than you having me arrested, I demand that you apologise to your men and to me for your attitude and action, otherwise I'll have you reported.'

When the officer saw the decoration he coloured up, stood to attention, saluted in the manner required towards those wearing the OBE decoration. He immediately without hesitation apologised both to George and the men and ordered them to dismiss. Later some of the men saw George in the town and thanked him for teaching the officer a much-needed lesson. They told him that this particular officer had been rather laying it on too thick of late. George advised them to keep quiet about the affair adding that, although he would do it again if the occasion arose, the decoration did not carry with it the authority he had bluffed their officer into believing it did, because it was a civil division award not a military one.

In the late summer of 1919, the father of the member of parliament for South Norfolk (Lord Cozens-Hardy) became very ill. It was feared he would not recover. In this event a by-election would become necessary as the present MP would be elevated to the peerage. The South Norfolk divisional party therefore began to prepare itself for another election campaign. Once more they invited George to be their prospective candidate. His health was still giving cause for concern, and he felt a younger man should be selected. In addition he had recently been elected chairman of Fakenham Parish Council and he thought it would be wiser to content himself by confining his interest at present in local affairs rather than those larger national issues. In view of his declining the invitation, the divisional party decided to hold the question in abeyance until 29 May 1920. A special meeting was then called and it was decided not to let the seat go uncontested should a by-election arise. Invitations were accordingly sent out to the agricultural workers union and local Labour Parties for nominations. Mr W.B. Taylor eventually being chosen.

Lord Cozens-Hardy died a month later and a by-election became necessary. Despite their earlier preparations and the choosing of a candidate, the party felt themselves not wholly prepared for the contest. They came to the reluctant conclusion that they must withdraw from the contest and concentrate their efforts upon preparing for the general election instead. Although their action caused delight within the opposition camp, who were already well advanced with their campaign, it caused great displeasure within the ranks of the agricultural workers union in the division. As a result, a letter was sent to the union executive by the branches demanding that a union candidate should contest the seat. If not, many said they would consider withdrawing from the union. The executive therefore called a conference, having realised how deeply its members felt on this issue. The conference consisted of delegates representing every branch in the South Norfolk division. The Norfolk members of the executive who attended were led by the president, Walter Smith. They had authority to act on behalf of the executive. The divisional Labour Party executive was also invited to attend.

The difficulties of nominating a candidate were outlined by the president. The delegates were then invited to express their views. One after another they declared it was their branches' view that the election should be fought. They were each sure that it could be won for Labour. Many of them emphasised that if nothing was done about contesting the seat they would feel the union had let them down, in which case they, the delegates, would not hold themselves responsible if their members left the union because of it. A resolution was then moved and immediately seconded, and carried unanimously that the union forthwith nominate a candidate. The divisional Labour Party would be asked to co-operate. When the president asked for nominations the delegates shouted as if with one voice: 'Our George!'.

George felt very embarrassed. He thanked them for the honour and trust thus shown for him, but pointed out his age and present state of health. He told them he thought this might prove a serious handicap to them, and under those circumstances he believed they would be better advised to seek a younger man. But the delegates replied that they believed him to be the only man who could win the seat for them, and if he would consent to stand they would do all they could to ease the strain for him. The president said he would assist him at his meetings and would see that he did not overtax his strength. Mr Gooch volunteered once more to act as his honorary agent, whilst Mr Taylor said he also would do all he could to help as much as if he had himself been the candidate. In face of all this enthusiasm George said he felt he could do no other than accept the invitation. They could rely upon him to do his best at all times to further the workers' interest. The delegates then rose to their feet and cheered him to the echo.

The election campaign had already been in progress a week which meant that George and his supporters had much leeway to make up. The election address was ready for print within twenty-four hours of the conference. It embraced the entire official Labour Party programme and his surprise entry into the fight caused some 'fluttering of the dove cotes' of the opposition camp. It was well known that he was the strongest possible candidate at that time who could be found to oppose them. George's supporters and colleagues were true to their word. They rallied around him as one man, helping him to surmount his physical difficulties. George Hewitt, Walter Smith and Edwin Gooch accompanied him to practically every meeting. In the background were numerous others quietly working for his victory. Amongst the most notable of these latter was the Earl of Kimberley. Everywhere throughout the constituency George was met with tremendous enthusiasm. Even the places where previously he had met with much bitter and hostile opposition he found he was now well received and given a good hearing.

It was with great confidence that he, accompanied by Elizabeth, his niece, and Walter Smith, went to the declaration of the poll at the Shire Hall, Norwich on 9 August 1920. The result proved that confidence fully justified.

The result was:

Edwards (Lab)	8,595
Batty (Coalition Lib)	6,476
Roberts (Ind. Lib)	3,788
Labour Majority	2,118

Numerous congratulatory telegrams awaited him on his return home to Fakenham. They came from all parts of the country, and even from some of his opponents who held him in high esteem. But it was really not until he was ready to make his journey to London to take his seat in parliament that the full impact of his new role and its responsibility came upon him. He was almost overcome with emotion. Elizabeth feared for a moment that his health was breaking down again, and inquired what was the matter. He replied, 'I wish my dear Charlotte could know of this happy day. I pray God keep me humble, that I might remain always the same George she knew, the agricultural labourer, and so prove loyal to my class.'

Elizabeth, Messrs Gooch, Taylor and Smith accompanied him to the Houses of Parliament. They had obtained tickets for the gallery so that they could witness him take the oath. At the appropriate time George was led by two supporters to the clerk's table where he took the oath and signed the roll. He then shook hands with the Speaker. Upon doing so he was greeted with cheers and the singing of the song 'To be a Farmer's Boy.' After signing the roll, George stepped back, quite unaware that the prime minister, Lloyd George, was close behind him, and he accidentally stepped upon his toe. The premier smiled as George apologising said: 'I do not expect it will be the last time I will tread on your toe.'

To George's great surprise upon his return home to Fakenham he found a great crowd of people awaiting his arrival at the railway station. They escorted him from the train to a wagonette they had brought and conveyed him to the Market Square, led by the Fakenham town band who played 'See the Conquering Hero Comes.' Cheering crowds lined the streets en route, and still more filled the Market Place and Square on their arrival there. It was estimated that there were about two thousand people. Speeches were then made by local trade unionists, church dignitaries and other local notable people representing most walks of life.

The adjournment of parliament on the 16 August did not bring him much respite or rest. He was determined not to neglect his local government work nor that of the chapel. With his election to parliament he found himself in great demand for special religious services in addition to those he normally took on his own home primitive methodist circuit. Then of course he felt duty bound to spend as much time as he could in his parliamentary constituency of South Norfolk, meeting the people and speaking at numerous meetings.

On 19 October 1920, the House re-assembled for the autumn session. It was two days later that George took the opportunity during the debate upon the unemployment question to make his maiden speech. He followed the minister of labour who had enlarged upon the present state of the unemployed. George began thus:

> I have listened very attentively to the speech of the Right Hon. Gentleman.
> I am not so much concerned with the description he gave us of the state of
> unemployment as I am with the fact that there are unemployed and a lack
> of provision made for them to find employment especially among ex-
> servicemen. I find that my Right Hon. friend is very anxious to lay the
> responsibility for the unemployment and lack of provision for the
> unemployed upon everyone except the government. He dealt with the
> housing question, and he made a great point of the fact that housing is
> being delayed in consequence of the conduct of the trade unionists in the
> building industry. But he did not tell the House that trade union workers in
> the trade offered that if the government will guarantee there shall be no
> unemployed in their trade they will remove the restrictions of which he
> complains.

George then described the situation in his own area:

> We decided to erect 250 houses. We prepared our plans and put out our
> contracts. We erected a number of houses for the working classes. We

were told by the government that in deciding on the rents we were to fix such a rent as we deemed reasonable according to wages earned in the district. We fixed the rents, as some of us think, rather too high. We had full local knowledge. We said that for a six-roomed house the rent should be £20 per year, with rates on top of that, and for a five-roomed house £14 per year, plus rates. What did the Minister of Health do? We sent him a return showing that the earnings of the agricultural labourers in the district average £2 6s per week, and those of other classes of workers £3 10s per week. The Minister came down on top of us and would not sanction the rents we had fixed. He demanded that the local authority should charge a man earning £3 10s per week £1 per week rent, and that for the five-roomed house 16s per week should be charged. Do the government imagine that any local authority, with its knowledge of the condition of things, would be content to erect houses and ask agricultural labourers with their wives and families to pay a rent of 16s per week out of a wage of £2 6s? Do they imagine that any local authority will erect houses for which they are to charge a man earning £3 10s per week £1 as rent? Do they imagine that out of the wages they are earning the men could pay such high rents as that? If they do, I can only suggest they should experiment on themselves for one month at least. This bombshell was thrown at the local authorities throughout the length and breadth of the country, with the result that they will not touch housing schemes until the Minister of Health abates his demands in this respect. I maintain that the responsibility for the delay in erecting houses falls directly upon the Government, but for whose action house building might have been proceeded with, and the present unemployment would not have grown to the extent it has.

George then turned to the question of the government's general attitude towards the agricultural industry saying,

I remember the time when there were 950,000 agricultural labourers and others employed on the land. At the present time there are only 550,000 so employed, and yet we have in my own county today 500 agricultural labourers standing by for want of work! I heard the question asked of the Minister of Health why this was so. I think I can give the reply. It is largely due to the gambling which is now going on in land. It is also due, in part, to bad farming which has been prevalent for many years that is responsible for the decrease in the number of men employed on the land. We ask the Government, as far as the land question is concerned, to do what they did during the war, namely to put into force the compulsory clauses of the Defence of the Realm Act. We have today, I believe, between 2,000,000 and 3,000,000 acres of land out of cultivation. We were told the other day that there were 800,000 acres less under wheat this year, and I believe I am correct in saying that since the armistice 80,000 acres of land have gone out of cultivation that were brought under cultivation during the war. Why do not the Government put into force the compulsory clauses and compel those who call the land theirs to keep it in cultivation?

He ended his speech with an appeal for government action in regard to re-afforestation and smallholdings schemes to help the plight of the ex-servicemen and their desire to keep farming:

In my own county we have 500 ex-servicemen who cannot get on the land, and we have spent all the money the government will let us have. I would make an appeal to the Right Hon. Gentlemen opposite and to the government to take this question seriously. I have spent fifty years of my life trying to upraise my class. I have endeavoured to exercise a moderating influence, and I think that up to the present I have been successful. No one can charge me with being an extremist. I want, however, to point this out to the government. Our influence over men and women may be lessened when they know that the barns are full and the cupboard is empty. Therefore, I ask them to use all powers they possess under the Defence of the Realm Act and to deal at once with this land problem. It can be dealt with at once. Set these men to work. We do not plead for doles; we do not plead charity. What we say is: 'In heaven's name, find them work!'

George sat down amidst loud applause from his side of the house. He had delivered his maiden speech in his true native Norfolk tongue and phrased it in terms that were in keeping with it; it really brought the countryside to the House of Commons - something which continued to draw members from both sides of the house to the chamber when he was speaking, and won for him their permanent respect. The autumn session proved a very strenuous one. It entailed long sittings, but George never missed one division. Often he never left the house for thirty-six hours, during which he went into the division lobby nearly thirty times against the Lord's amendments. Amongst the most notable bills before the house in which he was able to play a useful part was the Agriculture Bill. He spoke upon it several times and worked hard to get new clauses put in it to safeguard the land worker who lived in the tied cottage. In connection with this he had several interviews with Sir

Arthur Boscawen, the minister in charge of the bill. As a result, the workers were assured of compensation by way of one year's rent and removal expenses when compelled to leave their cottages at short notices. The tenant farmer, too, became assured of some security of tenure or compensation for disturbance. He was also granted a minimum price for his corn, and the wages board became re-established for four years. All in all no mean achievement for a 'new boy' to parliament. A view recognised when he was further honoured in being appointed a county alderman of Norfolk County Council. This office he held until his death.

Side by side with the growth of George's influence and work on behalf of the land workers was seen the growth of the union. The workers were becoming better organised and less afraid to demand better wages and conditions. These factors stirred the farming community to greater efforts to retard George's influence and destroy the growing power of the union. It was during his first few months in parliament that George had first become aware of efforts to discredit him. He was approached upon several occasions by wealthy opposition members who invited him to join them in drinks at high-class places. But these he consistently and firmly refused. He had taken note how some of his colleagues in the past had given way to similar temptations which had eventually led to them being discredited and to their downfall. No doubt there were also those amongst his own class who were somewhat envious and jealous of his growing influence, and whose feelings were easily played upon by his opponents. These feelings may have been encouraged when it was known that George was to be further honoured. It was announced in February 1921, that he had been invited by His Majesty King George V to attend a garden party at Buckingham Palace.

At the party George was presented to their majesties the King and Queen, after which the King expressed the desire to have further conversation with him. In the course of this conversation the King questioned George about his early life, particularly about his parents and their privations, and those George himself had suffered. His Majesty remarked, 'One of my own labourers brought up a family on thirteen shillings per week, but this is much worse.' Their Majesties appeared even more astonished as George told of his wife teaching him to read and of his giving up smoking to be able to buy books. The King then inquired whether or not the land workers were better off now. To which George replied that they were, but there was still much room for improvement for a good deal of privation still existed. The conversation then turned to the position of the workers upon His Majesty's Sandringham estate, the King suggesting that conditions there were more satisfactory. George agreed and said he desired to express appreciation of His Majesty's efforts in this respect. He added, 'If all other landlords followed the same lines there would be little trouble.' The conversation closed by their Majesties wishing George well in the future.

Soon after the press reports of his visit to Buckingham Palace, George began to receive numerous anonymous letters which accused him of being a traitor to his class. He found that reports were circulating in some of the villages that he had forgotten the workers since he could 'walk and talk with Royalty.' The suggestion of earlier years was again resurrected that George Edward's chief aim was to feather his own nest. Never was there a greater falsehood spoken or implied. In addition to these personal attacks, he soon became aware of yet another move to disrupt the union and divide the workers. Some farmers began to encourage workers from other trades and industry to work for them in their spare time. In particular this was the case with some railway men, whose own wages at that time were not very great. The temptation to add to their meagre income in their leisure hours was difficult to resist.

The agricultural workers' union sent a strong protest to the National Union of Railwaymen requesting them to do all they could to prevent their members from engaging in this practice which they considered assisted the farmers in their efforts to divide the workers and which led to many full-time men becoming discharged. The result of this protest was the following letter sent to the NUR branches by the then industrial secretary, C.T. Cramp:

For some time I have been receiving complaints from the Agricultural Labourers' Union and the British Gardeners' Association with reference to railwaymen working on the land after finishing their railway duties, some working for farmers, some doing gardening. This conduct is having a very detrimental effect on men who get their living in these occupations, and as the Agricultural Labourers' Union points out, so long as farmers can obtain casual labour they are enabled to keep down the wages of the agricultural labourer and also weaken their organisation. In addition to these complaints from these unions, I am receiving complaints from other unions respecting members of the NUR working in their spare time as musicians, painters etc, and the result is that a very bad feeling exists in some districts against the NUR and its members. I shall be glad if the officials and members of your branch will endeavour to stamp out this practice, as if this kind of thing continues, it will only bring division in the ranks of the labour movement where we should have united.[1]

Yet worse was to follow. As in Arch's day, so now again a rival union was set up which called itself the National Union of Landworkers. It was led by Sam Peel of Wells-next-the-Sea, one of George's late colleagues. The object, it was said, was to draw employers and employees together into one common cause. Sam Peel's action at this time caused George great sorrow. He felt deeply hurt that a colleague, whom he had thought a lot of, should have taken the action he did and to so badly represent his, George's aims. It took him a long time to get over it. But he did and was able to overcome his personal bitterness in a forgiving and friendly attitude towards Sam in his later days. In retrospect it must be said that Sam Peel, who in many ways made a positive contribution to the social welfare and education in Norfolk in his latter days, was a Quaker opposed to anything he believed would lead to strife. He sincerely believed that the farmers and farm workers could overcome their deep-rooted differences and join together in one organisation to pressurise the government to assist them in their economic differences. Sam sadly misjudged and misread the situation at that time. He became involved with well-to-do landowners and allowed himself to be compromised. The bitterness this caused lasted many years and was not easily forgotten.

At union meetings throughout Norfolk, George repeated his warnings of 1895. He pointed out the danger of this latest action of Sam Peel and the landowners. The object of which he said was to divide the workers. He made it clear that he did not wish to cause strife or bad feelings between employers and employees. He gave the farmers and landlords credit for being honest and sincere in their views, but at the same time he claimed the same for the workers. George inquired:

> How is it possible for workers and employers to have one object whilst the present social system remains and industry continued upon the principle of loss and profit? The workers have their views on the wage question; they claimed the right to obtain the highest value for the labour they give, that, is the starting point. But the farmers take the opposite view and they are bound to do so. They are bound to do so for they cannot look at the wage question from any other standpoint. The farmer has to buy his labour like everything else and therefore he endeavours to get it as cheap as he can. Where under this system can a common interest or object be found?

He then proceeded to remind his audiences of the experience of Arch's day how, when the rival unions had succeeded in smashing Arch's union, they too went out of existence. He demanded to know who was financing this new union. He said that if his suspicions were correct, it was the landlords. What object could his former colleagues have save only to divide the workers?

> If, they really desire to put the labourer upon his feet, why need they start another union to do it? The union I have founded has stood by you againstgreat odds for the past seventeen years, be loyal to it. It is dangerous to attempt to swap horses when crossing the stream.

Despite these warnings against the fifth columnists who led the rival union, many of the workers forsook George's union. The fifth columnists' task of persuading them that George and his colleagues had let them down was made easier by the general depression in agriculture at that time. The wages board had been abolished and wages were reduced from forty-six shillings to twenty-five shillings per week of fifty hours, but many were even paying much lower wages of twenty-two shillings and sixpence.

The general election of November 1922 came in the midst of these troubles and, as far as George and the union was concerned, added to them. In again being nominated as Labour candidate for South Norfolk, George soon realised that the divisions amongst the workers were being made full use of by his opponents. The forces of reaction were united against him. This had the effect of spurring him on rather than deterring him. He entered the conflict, despite these difficulties, full of hope and courage. He was ably supported by a devoted band of workers, led by a loyal colleague, Bob Watson who had recently moved from Walsingham to Wymondham to take up the duties of election agent. In addition to speaking each night in his own division, George found time to speak in support of his old friend and colleague, George Hewitt, who had been prominent in the St Faith's dispute who was contesting the neighbouring East Norfolk division. The forces arrayed against George proved too strong. The old game of divide and conquer by his opponents was effective as shown by the declaration of the election result on 16 November:

Maj. Hay (Unionist)	12,734
George Edwards (Labour)	10,159
Unionist majority	1,575

Once more we see George returning home a dejected man, wondering if his life's work had been in vain. However, his efforts did not pass entirely unnoticed or without appreciation. On 30 November, 1922, he was presented with a travelling bag on behalf of the Agricultural Workers' Union as a token of appreciation for his past and present work for the land workers. Also the Briton Bush Company of Wymondham had earlier presented him with a clothes brush.[2]

Notes

1. *Landworker*, 21 Jan. 1921.
2. The travelling bag is now an exhibit at the Gressenhall Rural Life Museum, Norfolk, and the clothes brush in the author's possession.

Chapter 8

The Norfolk Strike and the 'Travelling Bench'

George had vehemently opposed the repeal of the Agricultural Wages Board when he was in parliament. He had warned what the consequences would be for the farmer and the worker. The year 1923 saw the fulfilment of his prophecy. Depression throughout the industry again raised its ugly head. The workers' wages had already been drastically cut, further reductions were now once more being demanded. History seemed to be repeating itself. The whole countryside became a seething hotbed of discontent and unrest. Evictions and unemployment increased. The divisions among the land workers, caused by the rival union, appeared to be doing what it was expected they would, destroying any effective power of the official agricultural workers union on behalf of their members.

Although his defeat at the general election of 1922 had the immediate effect of leaving George bitterly disappointed and his faith sadly shaken, the plight of the land workers filled him with pity and sorrow. He began to ask himself whether or not he had been too hasty in blaming them for being so easily misled. Thus it is that we see him again rising to the challenge of the situation by re-entering the conflict against those who sought to beat the workers down. His endeavours to awaken the workers to their responsibility took the form of addressing union demonstrations throughout the length and breadth of the countryside, both weekdays and Sundays. In addition he wrote numerous letters to the press with the object of gaining public support for them. The fact that he addressed meetings on the sabbath was used by his opponents to turn would-be sympathisers within the church against him and the union. He was accused of desecrating the Lord's Day. But he was convinced that the labour movement was built upon the foundation of christianity. He sincerely believed he was equally serving God by preaching at union demonstrations which he interpreted to be Christ's gospel of *economic* freedom, as when he preached what he interpreted to be Christ's gospel of *spiritual* freedom in the pulpits of the church. It was because he held this view that he always insisted upon conducting the meetings for which he was responsible upon religious lines. He regretted very much that this practice ceased when he had no longer the responsibility for union meetings. Matters came to a head during February 1923 when the farmers requested a meeting of the Agricultural Conciliation Committee. They put forward a proposal of five pence per hour for a fifty-four hour week. The union representatives refused to accept this. A further offer was made of five pence half penny for fifty-four hours which the farmers insisted should be enforced. Following this the union executive agreed that if members were prepared to resist this they should be supported.

A great strike commenced in Norfolk as a result of a few farmers refusing to pay the national minimum wage. Their men were 'locked out'. It soon became apparent to the farmers that their action had stirred up a great resistance. They then made three more offers in succession which was twenty-four shillings for fifty hours, twenty-five shillings for fifty-two, and twenty-six shillings for fifty-four hours. However, the men in George's union had expressed the desire that if they were to fight they should fight for more than twenty-five shillings. They said they should make a move towards attaining the national minimum of thirty shillings for forty-eight hours. To do otherwise they said would lead to a worsening of their condition. The farmers, however, were adamant in their refusal to meet this demand and the strike spread throughout the county. As the strike dragged on many were the attempts to provoke the men. Farmers obtained fishermen and others to work for them. This was not always very successful from the farmers' view point in that problems arose from the inexperience of these men and gave their employers a few worrying and frustrating moments. One story tells of a farmer who had employed a fishermen and had difficulty in instructing him how to plough straight. He pointed to a cow that happened to be standing in a direct line in an adjoining field to that to be ploughed. The farmer said, 'Take that cow as your mark to follow.' Unfortunately the cow did not remain standing in that position, the fisherman, taking his boss's word literally with disastrous results in his ploughing.

Many police were drafted into the county when the authorities realised the sensitive nature of the situation as a result of so much blackleg labour being employed to do important work such as sowing the barley crop and ploughing, etc. They had also recruited pupils from distant places within the county and employed their own sons and daughters as well. Picketing became more aggressive. Some tyres on farmers' cars were slashed and some damage was done to overturned carts when horses set loose panicked. A farmer in the Erpingham area, near Cromer, had the army in to fetch straw for his animals and had a policeman to guard them. On one occasion he himself stood by with a gun. The policeman warned the strikers that the farmer might use his gun. But this did not deter them from rushing the farmer and setting the horses loose. They said: 'He'll have to shoot the lot of us to stop us.' The farmer soon scampered off. The strikers marched from village to village, calling the blacklegs to cease work. They demanded all workers to strike, even if their employer was paying the minimum wage. Only by a united effort they said would victory for all be achieved.

George saw the danger in the provocation of the men. He toured the length and breadth of the county urging them to be calm and not to give way to temper or to resort to violence which he said would only defeat their object and set the public against them. At many of the demonstrations at which he spoke he was carried shoulder high by the enthusiastic men who recognised him as their champion. Always he seemed to arrive at their rallies just at the right moment when feeling appeared to be mounting and likely to get out of hand. Nevertheless tensions rose dangerously high, particularly so in the areas around Fakenham, Walsingham and Wells. Here the farmers seemed to have been more fortunate, or otherwise, in obtaining blackleg labour. Added to this provocation was the fact that the leader of the rival union, Sam Peel, was holding meetings in an endeavour to persuade the workers not to strike. One such meeting was to be held at Wells. Sam had been successful in persuading a few to accept the farmers' promise of better wages and conditions when agriculture was put upon a firmer basis. So incensed were the strikers as a result of this that they threatened to break up Sam's Wells meeting and throw him into the harbour. George hearing this on his travels, hastily arranged a meeting at Wells which he addressed and so prevented any trouble. One of the lighter sides of the dispute is seen in the case of the parson of East Rudham inviting the strikers to his church each Sunday during the dispute, telling them if they came they could have the collection. They regularly turned up and, although there were some prominent farmers in the congregation, they were given the collection as promised which went into the strike fund.

George decided to concentrate his efforts within his home area where it appeared to him the greater danger from provocation was. He urged the men to have courage, patience and above all to remain calm however much they might be provoked. He felt assured they would follow his advice. Nevertheless it seemed the employers were determined in their efforts to turn public sympathy away from the workers and to discredit George and the union. Provocation became very intense. It was customary for countrymen to carry sticks cut from the hedge when walking the fields and lanes. The strikers followed this custom on their marches. When their enthusiasm or anger was aroused they would wave them in the air. It may well be that in some instances of extreme provocation that someone was hit. It was reported that four pupils who were working on Mr E.H. Ringer's farm at Rougham were attacked with cudgels when strikers let loose the horses. In any case the farmers saw in this a chance to accuse them of resorting to violence. Police presence added to the strikers' provocation. Some bad language was used when tempers became frayed. But it must be recorded that no serious violence or damage was caused to life or limb. Despite this, somehow or other their opponents in the Walsingham area managed to bring a charge against about a hundred men. They were summoned to appear before the court there on 16 March 1923.

The Walsingham bench consisted of farmers, landlords and Sam Peel, the rival union leader. Rumour had it that very stiff sentences were likely to be imposed. Some even said that the men might be sent to prison. George believed if this happened a riot and violent upheaval throughout the county would result. He immediately conferred with fellow Labour magistrates in Fakenham and other benches who, like himself, were county magistrates entitled to sit upon any magisterial bench within the county of Norfolk. He suggested to them that they should travel with him to the Walsingham Court to ensure the men received fair treatment. This they all agreed to do. Arriving at Walsingham they found the village packed with a multitude of workers converging on the court house. They were shouting and calling for the blood of the rival union leader, the landowners and farmers. George feared that the magistrates had forestalled them by getting the men's cases over earlier than anticipated. But to his relief he learned that this was not so. He hastily addressed the crowd, imploring them to keep calm. He assured them that he and his fellow magistrates had come to see that justice was done. When they heard this, the crowd ceased their threatening manner and cheered him and his colleagues, singing 'For he's a jolly good fellow'.

Entering the court, George and his colleagues were greeted with suspicion and surly looks from the local magistrates. One demanded, 'What right have these fellows here?' This person happened to be a city magistrate whom George knew had recently moved to the area, and as a city magistrate had not so much right as George and his colleagues had to be present. He quickly pointed out this and said: 'We've come to see justice done.' This quelled any further opposition to their presence.

It soon became apparent that the local magistrates were determined to impose stiff sentences on the men. George and his colleagues opposed this, pointing out that no serious violent action had taken place and no one in this case had been hurt. It had been admitted that foul language was used and the police insulted and abused under provocation. George insisted this did not warrant stiff sentences. Furthermore, George warned the bench that the consequences of unjust sentences would be on the magistrates' own heads. After much discussion the magistrates not being persuaded to grant an acquittal, imposed a nominal fine of nine shilling per man. Meanwhile outside, rumour had it that Sam Peel had supported a severe sentence. Sensing the danger of such a rumour causing roused anger, George insisted on leaving the court with Sam to ensure no harm came to him. Sam, with other magistrates, was then able to leave by a back way through the Abbey grounds. Some rotten fruit was thrown at them, but they escaped unharmed. Meanwhile George got to the pump opposite the court house and again addressed the crowd, urging them to keep calm. So eventually, the crowd although being joined by many more men who had come late from the Egmere and Creake areas, dispersed quietly.

The late Eric Seaman of Walsingham, who was a young schoolboy at the time, has related how he played truant from school that day to see what was happening at the court house. He stood by the pump when George came out and held his coat while he addressed the crowd. A press photographer took a photograph of George and the crowd and it was in the paper the next day. On Eric's return to school next morning the headmaster enquired of him where he had been the previous day. Eric said he had been at home looking after his brother whereupon the headmaster produced the press photograph and said, 'Well, what's this?' Poor Eric was found out and caned.

In these days of massed flying pickets, as seen in the miners' strike 1984-85, one is apt to forget how near to a situation of violence and riot things came in Norfolk during the great strike of 1923. Undoubtedly the action George and his colleagues took that day in Walsingham prevented the outbreak of violence and bloodshed. Nevertheless his opponents made an effort to get him censured for attending the Walsingham court. The matter was raised on their behalf with the Lord Chancellor who replied that county magistrates had authority to travel to neighbouring benches, but that in such cases as that of Walsingham discourtesy might be shown by visiting magistrates if not invited so to do. Unfortunately, George appears to have been rather carried away by the success of the 'travelling bench'. At a union demonstration shortly after he gave way to the temptation to boast about it, threatening to use the same method again if the need arose. This being reported, he received the following letter from the Lord Chancellor's office, dated 18 September 1923.

> I am directed by the Lord Chancellor to inform you that his attention has been drawn to a statement which you are reported to have made in a speech at a recent meeting at Walsingham. In the course of the speech, you are reported as having said, 'no doubt you well remember the moving bench during the strike which paid a surprise visit to Walsingham. Well, I wish to issue a warning that if these ejectment orders continue to be granted, the travelling bench of magistrates will take place again - not ten this time, but twenty. We cannot get turned out because we have been appointed for the County of Norfolk.'
>
> The Lord Chancellor desires me to ask if the extract from the report I have quoted is correct.
>
> I am to say that his Lordship had recently under consideration cases in which magistrates in Norfolk without invitation, attended the sitting of Benches other than those to which they are normally attached. His Lordship directs me to enclose an extract from a letter which he caused to be sent to the Clerk of the Justices of the Tunstead and Happing Division in one of those cases and to the magistrates in question. In consequence of this letter the magistrates refrained from sitting on a Bench to which they were not attached. I am to add that the Chancellor would take a most serious view of the conduct of a Justice or a group of Justices who took such action as is described in the report of the speech which I have quoted, and that he would not hesitate to take such steps as seemed to him to be necessary to put an end to such conduct; but he feels sure that on reflection, and having regard to the considerations set forth in this letter, you will be able to give him an assurance that no such action is seriously contemplated by you.

The enclosed extract of the letter referred to above read as follows:

> The Lord Chancellor regards it as of the greatest importance that the arrangements which ordinarily prevail in Counties, whereby the sittings of the Bench in a particular Petty Sessional Division are attended only by certain specified Justices, should be maintained. The attendance of a Justice, who usually sits in one Petty Sessional Division, at the sitting of the Bench of another Division causes much administrative confusion. Furthermore, when any magistrate so attends for the purpose of hearing a

particular case, other evil consequences may follow. A suspicion may be engendered in the public mind that the magistrates so attending is influenced by some interest or prejudice on one side or the other of the case to be heard; grave doubts as to the impartiality of the Justices may thereby be aroused; and serious injury may be caused to the administration of justice as a whole.

George replied to this by return of post. It shows in admitting the correctness of the newspaper report of his speech that he nevertheless felt justified in making it and no real regret for it for the reason which he defines in his reply as follows exactly as he wrote it:

Yours of the 18th as directed by the Lord Chancellor will you kindly inform his Lordship that I have no doubt but what I was correctly reported at a recent meeting. I would, however, like to remind his Lordship, he having been a Politician know that things are very often said of which the speaker on the moment of excitement which in calmer moments know he will not put into practice and it was so in this case. I would like if I may remind his Lordship that there is always two sides to a question and it is so in this case. The Magistrates who visited the Walsingham Bench at the meeting you refer to the fact that they felt and the Public felt that these poor people who were summoned before the various Benches in Norfolk were not having justice meted out to them and further they were being tried and convicted by employers of labour who were affected by the strike like the Tunstead and Happing division the Chairman of that Bench own men on strike and it was only after he promised not to sit on the cases coming before the Bench that the Magistrates in question refrained from sitting. I would also like to remind his Lordship that there is at the moment some gross cases of hardship being inflicted on a good many of these poor men. Magistrates are granting ejectment orders and men are being turned out of their homes who have lived in them for years and are of the most exemplary character and in a number of cases the houses are still standing empty this was which I had in my mind when I made the speech your Lordship refers to. Not that I intended to carry out but to stop if possible by my influence what the general public believe is unjust and I can assure his Lordship there is a very strong feeling in this County that these poor men are being most unjustly victimised and if his Lordship could do anything by influencing the various Magistrates in the County to well look into every application for ejectment orders before granting them he would greatly allay the feeling that exist. I can however assure him so far as the Labour magistrates in the County is concerned we have no intention to repeat the Walsingham incident whatever we say on the platform in the moment of heat. But we do feel that a great deal of hardship is being inflicted on these people we shall however adopt another course by having the whole question raised in the house of Commons also in the House of Lords.

The great Norfolk strike ended by the workers returning to work at the rate at which they had come out. The farmers' leaders signed an agreement that no one should be victimised. George advised the workers and their employers to cease from hurling abuse at each other.

> No doubt, statements were made on both sides during the course of the dispute that in our calmer moments we may well think would have been better left unsaid. This, however, always happens in moments of excitement, during industrial and political controversy. But it is reflection of this sort that makes it more than ever necessary when the fight is over that we should all shake hands, and be friends, and that peace and goodwill should dwell among us.

With the advance of the year 1923, the days of the great Norfolk strike gradually receded into the past. George saw that, although the workers' loyalty and solidarity in their resistance to the attempts made to worsen their conditions had been successful, the fight was far from over. The farmers' agreement not to victimise the strikers was soon broken. They refused to reinstate some of their best men, many of whom had been in their employ from ten to forty years. Eviction from their homes was prevalent again. The leaders of the rival Landworkers' Union remained busy in their attempt to draw the workers from George's union. They had joined forces with the farmers and landlords in advocating the formation of a United Agricultural Party. Their policy was to be the abolition of Free Trade by the institution of protection with a duty on barley. In addition these rival union leaders claimed to represent the members at secret meetings and conferences that were held with the farmers to discuss wages and complaints that costs were high in view of the present rate.

Not all farmers supported the method and policy of their leaders, nor had they much faith in or time for the men who led the rival workers union, as the following extract from a letter to George from one such farmer shows. After reminding George of his approach to him in Norwich some three years since when he predicted a great depression in agriculture, and that he had then suggested to George that his party should join the National Farmers'

Union for political purposes because he felt this was the only means of saving village life from the poverty of years ago, the farmer wrote:

> Now that we are on the threshold of seeing that prediction (i.e. the agriculture depression) fulfilled, I appeal to you once again, on my own initiative and as a private individual for no one knows that I have this in my mind. But as a Christian like yourself knowing somewhat of poverty of our villages years ago, and again like yourself I have been watching every opportunity to help the raising of the status of the village life. ... Now I believe that something can be done even at this eleventh hour if we are politically united. That is not only those engaged immediately in agriculture but all that live and are interested in village life for we are all more or less depending upon each other ... I know such a movement will have to face many difficulties from both sides, but I am sure of this, that we should have an enormous following from all quarters ... I never saw so much interest and sympathy shown by the majority of farmers towards their employees as today, in fact there would have been an attempt an another very drastic cut had it not been for the many who hate the idea of paying their men a starvation wage.

The farmer ended his letter requesting an opportunity to meet George soon to exchange views on the subject. The following extract from his reply is interesting being advocated by some of his leaders in so much that he would be prepared, if he felt it necessary to take up an independent line. He wrote, after thanking the farmer for his letter:

> I will say it contains much that I am heartily in accord with ... The Government must at once come to the relief of agriculture if it is to be kept alive. I think the only difference that exist between myself and the Farmers' Union on this point is the form in which the relief should take, they will insist on advocating some kind of a system of Protection which in my judgement is a most clumsy way. You cannot have a tax or duty on one article alone, if we are going in for Protection then we must go the whole way and that would spell disaster and the farmers would be the first to lose and heavily by having to pay a higher price for their feeding stuffs and all their machinery, implements and tools ... I stand where I have always stood that is for the replacement on the Statute Book of the 1920 Act. I don't mind whether the relief is given by guarantee or by a bounty on all cereals grown. I think a bounty would be the best method, at the same time I should want the replacement of the Wages Board, for if we are going to protect one class in the industry we must also protect the weakest class. That, however, seems to be a bone of contention.

George then pointed out that with regard to the two organisations uniting, the difficulties previously existing when they had discussed it had been greatly intensified by the recent farm dispute and the spirit of revenge still apparent as reflected by the fact that many men were still locked out and being turned out of their homes.

> I might say, that I have strong faith if I had been in the House I could have prevented that dispute by bringing pressure upon the Government to do something for agriculture. It is not generally known when I found the Government were playing with the question and would not move I suggested to several of the leading farmers that we should have a friendly strike or in other words a united strike and force the hands of the Government, then would have been the time for a united policy, but they would not ... Do you think, dear friend that your people would be more willing to co-operate on a political basis more than they have been in the past, will not they still stand by their old Tory party? ... Still if anything could be reasonably done to benefit the industry as a whole I should be quite willing to co-operate. If I live to contest South Norfolk again I shall have my own agricultural policy irrespective of party which will be on the lines I have suggested.

It is not difficult to see why some of George's closest friends became a little impatient with him over his apparent tolerant attitude towards their opponents and employers. Added to this was what appeared to be a conceited view of his influence in high places and obstinate adherence to an independent agricultural viewpoint, which caused them to fear he was going a little too far.

The continued action within a rival union by some of his former colleagues greatly appalled and hurt George, especially as it was clear the real aim of the employers was an all-out effort to reduce wages. He reminded the employers that during the Norfolk strike they had promised to pay the workers more should the Rating Bill become law to de-rate their property. Now, although it had been passed they still complained about the wages they were called upon to pay. He warned them to think twice before making another attempt to reduce wages. So George continued his appeals to the land workers to stand firm against the rival union to remain loyal to their own union which had proved itself to represent their truest aspirations. In urging them to strengthen their organisation so they could more effectively combat all opposition, he said, 'I must renew my efforts to continue the flight, standing loyally by the side of my younger colleagues to stamp out this spirit of oppression, and the men themselves must buckle on the armour.'

In the midst of these worrying and anxious times, on 14 November 1923, a similar blow befell him as that which occurred in 1912 when Charlotte had died. His niece, Elizabeth, died of the same dread disease of cancer. She had been his loyal companion, nursed him through many a trouble since 1912, and like her aunt had taken a prominent part in local public work with her uncle. She had born her acute suffering and faced various operations very bravely until at last being compelled to give up all public work and become confined to her bed. When the end was near she called George to her side saying: 'Do not give up, uncle. Right will triumph in the end. Victory will crown your efforts. Give my love to all my friends and tell them to love God.' With these words she passed away. This bereavement greatly affected George's own health. However, he faced up courageously and was able to attend the funeral. It was rarely that such a funeral had been witnessed in Fakenham before. Hundreds of people of all shades of religious and political thought came from far and wide to pay their last respects to a great woman and to show their sympathy for a great man whom she had served so loyally. The service was held in the Buckenham Memorial Methodist Church and was conducted by the Revd A.B. Gowers, who paid tribute to her Christian character and public work with that of her uncle. Following the internment, George broke down, the reaction set in and he was confined to his bed for the next few days.

When George's health had similarly broken down following Charlotte's death, Elizabeth had come to look after him. He was greatly helped to overcome the despair his grief had brought him. Now following the loss of Elizabeth, again being stricken by grief, yet another loving and kind woman came to his aid. It was Miss Lucy Myers (later Mrs W. Dalton, who died 12 July 1969, aged 83). It was she who had nursed Elizabeth during the last few months of her illness. She felt very deeply for George in his grief, and readily agreed to stay on as his housekeeper and to mother the youngest of Elizabeth's children (the author of this book), whom George had adopted as his son, arranging that he should take his surname. Elizabeth had three other children, two girls and a boy. After Elizabeth lost her husband, the younger girl had gone to live in Lancashire with her mother's sister who had no children of her own. The elder girl had started work in the local Co-op shop and the son was studying for the teaching profession. However, some time

5. Sir George gardening at Queen's Road, Fakenham in 1924.

after the mother's death the elder daughter, through George's help, was able to train as a nurse (like her mother) at the Royal Free Hospital, London. The son also decided to seek a fresh career in Lancashire. Thus Lucy Myers (Aunt Lucy as she became known in George's household) was able to devote her whole attention to looking after George and his adopted son. It was not long before her gentle nursing and kindness brought George back to health and strength sufficient to enable him to take up his public work once more.

Chapter 9

Parliament Again

George's recovery coincided with the preparations for a general election. He received in December 1923, an invitation to once more contest the South Norfolk constituency on behalf of Labour. Although not feeling physically up to the task he allowed himself to be persuaded. As at the last election his opponent was Major Hay. It seemed clear that the treatment the land workers had received, and were still receiving, from the employers had hardened their attitude. A new spirit was abroad. George soon found himself as before surrounded by a loyal band of workers, led by Bob Watson and Edwin Gooch. Their enthusiasm spread to every worker throughout the division. All meetings were well attended. Various prominent Trade Union and Labour men came to support him, notably George Lansbury.

To emphasise his qualifications and worthiness to represent the people of South Norfolk, a pamphlet was issued in which George outlined his life story. To this his agent had added in large bold print:

Who could represent a Norfolk division better than the man who has lived his life as an agricultural labourer amongst Norfolk men? A man who knows by experience the bitter struggle and hardships that have been the labourer's lot.

Vote for Labour's emancipation, and make George Edwards MP.

George toured the whole of his division on polling day. He still, however, found time to hurry home to Fakenham to record his vote for his friend Noel Buxton, the North Norfolk constituency Labour candidate. Returning later to his own constituency, he was greeted in many of the villages by bands of workers marching to record their votes. They told him they were not going to ride to the poll with the Tories.

At the close of the poll George retired to his friend's home in Wymondham for the night to await the declaration the next day. That night he had a strange experience. It seemed as if in a dream Elizabeth, his niece, came to his side and whispered: 'Sleep well, Uncle, you have earned your rest, you have won by hundreds.' He awoke next morning feeling on top of the world. His confidence was clearly shown in his whole bearing as he greeted his friends and his agent, Bob Watson, later at the count. They themselves were feeling rather anxious and were much surprised by

George's bidding them 'Cheer up, we're in by hundreds!' And so the final
figures proved to be the case:

Edwards	11,682
Hay	10,821
Majority	861

Upon his return to Wymondham after the declaration, he was given a
wonderful reception. A huge crowd, headed by the New Buckingham brass
band, awaited him. His car was quickly roped and drawn to the Fairland Hall
by scores of joyous men. There another large crowd awaited him, so many
were there that the hall could not contain them all. Speeches were made by
the divisional labour and trade union leaders, among whom was the late
Lord Kimberley. Arriving later at his home at Fakenham he learnt that not
only had his friend Noel Buxton been returned as the member of North
Norfolk, but also that throughout the country sufficient of his labour
colleagues had been returned to form the first Labour government.

It was with a feeling of great pride that George took his seat in
parliament again. Particularly was this so as on this occasion it was not on
the opposition benches but that of the new Labour government. Although the
cause he represented was the government of the day, he was soon to realise
that the troubles of the workers were not over yet. Many of the reforms he
and his colleagues and their party had hoped to see enacted as indicated in
their election programme, were prevented by the combination of the Tory
and Liberal party members. Not having an overall majority, the government
was a minority government. The average worker could not understand this.
Consequently when their troubles and difficulties were not immediately
eased with the return of the Labour government they became critically
apathetic. The government's opponents inside and outside parliament
naturally made full use of this state of affairs. They accused the Labour Party
of deceiving the workers and of breaking their promises.

In common with other Labour MPs, George became a target for severe
criticisms. He was surprised and not a little hurt by a critical article by his
colleague of the early days of his Union, Sir Richard Winfrey, which
appeared in a local paper. This article conveyed an undercurrent, probably
not really meant, of innuendo passing reflection not only upon the Prime
Minister, but also upon Noel Buxton, Walter Smith and George:

> To start with there is my friend Mr Noel Buxton as Minister of
> Agriculture. What could be more interesting than to watch Mr Buxton's
> handling of the agricultural situation? Mr Buxton and I have been friends
> and colleagues for several years, he as Member for North Norfolk and I
> for the adjoining constituency of South-West Norfolk. We have been on
> many platforms together, and I should say, think alike on many subjects

Then why, may be asked, are we in different camps? Well, it was largely, I fancy, a matter of tactics with Mr Buxton; he could foresee the Labour Party in Norfolk would have their eye on his seat. Indeed they threatened to fight every seat in Norfolk, and so at his election quietly declared themselves as converts to Labour. George Edwards, who lives in the constituency and is father of the Agricultural Labourers' Union and always friendly with Mr Buxton (indeed, he has good reason to be) sanctioned Mr Buxton's astute move. And so we have the same man with the same ideals under another flag. Mr Buxton's agent carried over with him the Liberal organisation and there it was - fait accompli - a safe Liberal seat become, by a stroke of manoeuvring, a Labour seat. I remember George Edwards pointing this out to me with great glee and saying 'Why don't you do as Buxton has done?' My reply was 'But I cannot subscribe to the capital levy or the nationalisation of industries. Has Mr Buxton subscribed to these?' 'Ah,' said George with a twinkle in his eye, 'We have not pressed Mr Buxton to define his views on these matters yet, he is heart and soul with the agricultural labourer and in favour of a Wages Board, and that is enough for us at present.'[1]

The rest of the article endeavoured to prove the inconsistencies of the whole Labour party and government by the fact of its being made up with such men differing on fundamental principles and policy. George replied to this in various speeches he made, declaring that the statements Sir Richard had made in the article, especially as relating to himself, were untrue and were designed to throw a red herring across the path of the workers.

In addition to this criticism by a former colleague, George found he had also to face a campaign to label his Labour colleagues and himself as 'Bolsheviks,' inferring they were allied to the communists and supporters of the Russian form of a socialist state. At a labour party garden fete in his constituency at Wymondham during the summer months, he took the opportunity with Miss Dorothy Jewson (MP for one of the Norwich constituencies who opened the fete) to answer some of these accusations. Miss Jewson had recently returned from a visit to Russia. She gave a brief account of her experience there. She told her audience that much had been written about the Russian government, but much had been lies. She admitted the Russian government was not ideal and that it was a dictatorship which it was seditious to criticise. She reminded that in England not so long ago people had been imprisoned for criticising a capitalist government. Neither form of government was the type the Labour party wished to see. George, following up Miss Jewson's speech, said,

> Miss Jewson's experience disclosed quite a different condition from the tale the yellow press gave this country. Before I went to the Trades Union Congress at Hull I was nervous because I had read in one paper that we

were going to have in our midst the awful Russian representatives. It was suggested that the Congress during the week would be no better than an asylum, that not a building would be left standing in Hull at the end of the week and that all the delegates would be flying at each other's throats. The Russian delegates were there and received from their English fellows the welcome they deserved. The Russian delegates would go back to their country full of encouragement, whatever the capitalists would do in this country.

At this time George also found himself assailed not only by political opponents but also by some members of his own church. These mainly criticised him for his continued support of his union's Sunday demonstrations. Letters attacking him on this issue appeared not only in the local press but also in the official publication of the Primitive Methodist Church, *The Primitive Methodist Leader*. Among letters in the press were those of a Wesleyan Methodist minister and from one who signed himself 'Veritas'. There was another from one who signed himself 'An Agricultural Worker' saying,

> Mr Edwards justifies his action on the score that Labour is Christian, and clearly implies that Labour is the only party that can truly claim that name ... that a man of Mr George Edwards' experience should adopt the viewpoint is amazing in the extreme ... We are persuaded that in this matter he is rendering a grave disservice to the cause he has at heart, and making far more difficult the task of hardly pressed workers in our village churches, who in unobtrusive ways are rendering service of first-rate importance to the community.

Another wrote:

> One of the most objectionable features about these so-called Labour-Christian or Christian-Labour meetings is the manner in which the speakers, who are professedly Christian men, most unwarrantably drag our Lord Jesus into their political theories, and make Him to appear to be a partaker of their view! ... It is astounding that a man like George Edwards should lend himself to such a plan of securing or maintaining political support by such an unfounded doctrine.'

The effect of this kind of criticism so disturbed him that George offered his resignation both as a member of the Primitive Methodist Church and as a local preacher. But his many influential friends within that church, and those of his own local church who held him in high regard, persuaded him not to take such a drastic step. Among those who sought to turn him against the step of resignation was the then editor of *The Primitive Methodist Leader*, the Revd George Bennett. He wrote:

> Please do not pursue the purpose you intimate in your letter. Such a course would grieve your friends, and they are very many more than you

imagine. I am deeply convinced that for you to go forward in your general work will be the best, both for yourself and for the work of the Kingdom.

George accepted this advice. He withdrew his threat to resign and continued his membership and active work as a preacher in the Primitive Methodist Church. He soon found that he was in increasing demand both for his own and other churches so that with his parliamentary and constituency duties he was fully occupied with little or no spare time. Despite this he did not forget or neglect his union. He spoke at many of its demonstrations in different parts of the country.

His last term in parliament, whilst only lasting a few months, proved a most strenuous one, more so than that of his first parliamentary experience. There were many late sittings with prolonged debates which were caused by the persistence of the opposition. After one of these late sittings George was returning to his lodgings when he slipped on the pavement, hitting his head upon the kerb. He lost consciousness and was taken to a nursing home. It was thought his heart was affected by the overtaxing of his strength by the long hours of concentration and other duties of his busy parliamentary life. He also suffered concussion in his fall. His enforced stay for the next few days probably gave him the opportunity of a much-needed rest. Upon leaving the nursing home he felt a new man once more.

George had become known in his locality as the poor man's lawyer. Often after a heavy week in Westminster and a tiring train journey home, he would have just sat down to enjoy his evening meal (which in the cold weather would be hot onion gruel that he still enjoyed, believing it kept the cold out) when someone would call to seek his advice. He would leave his meal or whatever he was doing to see them. He never turned anyone away. However, it was not always the poorer classes that sought his advice. A local farmer regularly called on a Saturday evening. Despite their political differences, George always made him welcome, listened to his problems and grievances and frankly gave his opinion and advice upon them. The farmer said he appreciated being able to talk with George. It helped to lift the worries from his mind for he trusted George. His advice was sound. It was a tribute that he treasured, coming from one whose politics so greatly differed from those of his own. In addition to the people who called personally to seek his advice there were the numerous letters from all kinds of folk, with a vast range of problems. He endeavoured to answer them all himself, but they continued to increase so much that it became impossible for him to do so. Lucy Myers therefore had to help him to ensure each and all got a reply. Not all the letters were advice-seeking, and not all contained adverse criticism. His work for the poor and his victory over great personal hardships in his early days had become known far and wide, even outside the British Isles.

He was greatly cheered and encouraged one day by receiving a letter from a lady in Melbourne, Australia who had read of his early boyhood struggles and his progress to national recognition by his efforts on behalf of the poor.

There were times when George doubted the wisdom of the Labour party accepting office as a minority government. However, after seven or eight months of its term of office he told his supporters in his constituency of South Norfolk, that having now seen some of the results of the government, headed by its prime minister, Ramsay MacDonald, he was of the opinion that it had done the right thing. He said,

> If the government came to the country before Christmas it would be with a good record. They had removed the suspicion to which the country had been regarded by other countries and had re-established the credit of the country in the eyes of other nations. The Labour government had fulfilled its promise to the labourers, and the Wages Board would enable the labourers to get a higher wage without taxing foodstuffs. As soon as the Norfolk Wages Committee is constituted I expect the labourers representatives to go in for a five-shilling increase at once.

Despite his outward optimism, and his faith in his party's ideals and leaders, he was nevertheless sure that the government would be forced to come to the country before the Christmas of 1924. Inwardly he, too, felt that the fight to retain his parliamentary seat and also that the fight to ensure a return of a Labour government would be more than difficult. No doubt he was aware that his continued advocacy for the acceptance by the farming community of a system of co-operative farming and his condemnation of them for their failure to do so, together with his support for a more friendly attitude and a treaty with, and loan to Russia would be weighted heavily against him by his political opponents in the election campaign. With these things in mind he said,

> I wish the tenant farmers would be reasonable. They asked for credit and when the Government gave it to them at 4 per cent instead of 6 per cent they said it was no use to them. If they had started the co-operative societies that the Government was anxious to help them with there would have been no trouble over the milk business - it would have been better for consumers and producers alike.

He then went on to urge his supporters to be ready for the general election,

> In 1922 I was called a Bolshevist. It was said that I was a believer in the nationalisation of women, and anti-Christian. The same thing will be said again, so be prepared for it!

By the autumn the opposition were able to force a general election. This took place on the 29 October 1924. This time the South Norfolk Tories nominated Mr J.A. Christie. He was a very highly respected employer and a member of the Norfolk County Council, one for whom George and his colleagues had high regard. They knew he would make a good and formidable opponent who would himself fight a clean campaign. Unfortunately this was not the case with some of Mr Christie's supporters who failed to follow his example. Distasteful tactics and unpleasant propaganda were used. Some tried to prove George's efforts and ideals on behalf of the agricultural worker would lead to the ruin of the industry. It was implied that the policy George and his party advocated would result in arable farming becoming impossible. There would be less piecework and no harvest money. It was said that old hands would find themselves stood off. The inference was that George and his fellow trade unionists within the Labour party were irresponsible. As was expected, much was made of the Russian 'red bogey'. He was labelled a disciple of revolution. The following is a sample of some of the literature distributed by his opponents:

LOOK OUT FOR THE 'RED' MAN FROM MOSCOW

Do you know that the Communists, who are advanced Socialists under another name, have started a campaign among you? And do you know that these people seek to bring about a civil war and revolution in Great Britain? Have you spotted these revolutionary agents yet, or so far, have they been too clever for you?

They were to be found in many districts as extra harvesting hands, or as the men and women who come to help in the hay-making, the sowing, the threshing, or the hundred other jobs for which extra hands are employed. They are all trained agitators who at some time or other have had experience on farms, but afterwards went into the factories in the city and have learned to spread Communism there, to foment strikes and that sort of thing.

They begin by urging you to vote 'Labour', promising you better wages and working conditions under a 'Labour' Government. This is only to get your good-will. In time they will preach open revolution to you. Already in some districts country workers are being formed into clubs, and plans are now ready for these clubs to welcome and be welcomed by Communist clubs in big cities, in order to spread and strengthen the movement. Communist parties are gradually being built up in rural areas, and the men and women are being organised as carefully as the other workers in the factories. And all to help on Civil War and Revolution. This is why you are so important to them. Only when you have been 'converted', will the Communists be able to bring the Revolution down from the cities to the rural areas: only then will they be able to capture the most important strongholds, and not until they have captured those will they make sure of a food supply in the days of the Revolution.

Before very long they are going to appeal to the small farmer and the
market gardener, but you are the main objective at the present. Don't think
that because you belong to a Trade Union that is enough. Your trade union
is being undermined and plotted against. So are all other Unions, and very
successfully too. An active fight against these revolutionary agents is the
only means of safety. And remember that a Conservative party, such as the
Conservative and Unionist Party, is the greatest enemy of Communism.[2]

Amongst the few anonymous letters he received at this time was one
enclosing a copy of his parliamentary speech on the Land Bill's third reading
debate on 25 November 1920. Across this the writer had written in large
capitals AGITATOR AND STRIKE MAKER and at the foot of the paragraph of
that speech in which George had said that the agricultural labourers
demanded wholeheartedly that the Bill should become law, the anonymous
writer had written 'And get unemployment and lower wages.' In pasting this
into his scrapbook George wrote upon it: 'Sent to me be some blackguard
Tory. I pity their ignorance.'

Obviously he was deeply hurt by these accusations and abusive
anonymous letters, but kept his feelings to himself. He was unwilling to take
any outward action, save only to concentrate on preparing his election
campaign and address, which he felt sure would adequately answer all his
critics. It took the form of a complete analysis of the Labour government's
work, ideals and achievements during its nine months in office.
Endeavouring to explain in simple language why more progressive
legislation could not be fulfilled, he wrote:

> It must be remembered that Labour members in the last Parliament did not
> number one in each three of the members. It has been our purpose not to
> throw in the face of Parliament proposals which, beforehand, we knew
> would be rejected, but to secure in the term of a first session some results,
> which would make an impression for good upon the lives of people who
> are most in need. Accordingly, the position of the unemployed has been
> improved; an approach has been made towards a full measure of justice
> for the Aged Poor; plans have been put through, which will speedily
> reduce the grievance of thousands of people anxious to secure better
> homes. In the service of Agriculture and of Education notable headway for
> improvement has been made, and in the varied provisions of a striking and
> beneficent Budget a Labour Chancellor has shown a mastery in finance
> never excelled in recent years ... The Government has fulfilled its pledges
> to the labourers and the National Agricultural Wages Board is an
> accomplished fact. The Coalition Government abolished the Wages Board
> and left the farm worker without protection. The Labourers of South
> Norfolk know to their cost what followed. After a hard struggle the
> Labour Government's Wages Bill has become an Act, and the machinery

for legally regulating the labourer's wage is about to be set in motion. Under this Act the labourer of South Norfolk can obtain and maintain a decent standard of life.

However, the strength of his opponents and the subversive propaganda had its effect upon the electorate despite his gallant effort. The declaration of the poll showed a victory for George's Tory opponent. The Tory Party also now became the government. The votes cast were:

J A Christie (Con)	14,189
George Edwards (Lab)	11,376
Tory Majority	2,813

The manner of his defeat at this election, at the age of seventy-four, would have caused many a younger man to have given up all public work and to have retired to a quieter home life. But not so for George. He realised of course that this last defeat meant the end of his parliamentary work and within a year he officially resigned as a parliamentary candidate. But because he felt sure the advent of another Tory government would bring added difficulties to the workers, particularly the land workers, he decided, when sufficiently recuperated from the 'wounds' of electoral defeat, to concentrate his efforts to ease the lot of the workers more in the local sphere of his town and county. He was also sure that much effort would be needed by the local and divisional Labour parties and his union to overcome the setbacks the result of the election had brought them. He therefore offered his help in organising and preparing for the next general election, both in North Norfolk and South Norfolk constituencies.

The task was far from easy. Misrepresentation of his motives continued to be bandied about. The general apathy of those he tried to help was one of the most difficult things to face. Then there were the abusive letters which continued to arrive, most of which were anonymous. It made him wonder whether after all he had done the right thing in continuing in public work, and left him feeling depressed. Yet he was at most times able to see the humorous side in them and concluded that they were the result of much stupidity and ignorance which had to be overcome. But it was encouraging to him that amongst the correspondence received there were those that took the trouble to let him know they valued and appreciated his life's work. One such was:

> My father was an agricultural labourer in East Norfolk and we have followed very closely your efforts to better the conditions of the land workers, we are proud of you and altho' we never met you, my sister and I would be delighted to have your photo to hang by the side of Keir Hardie. I will pay all necessary expense for same if you could let us have one.

Early in September 1925, The Trades Union Congress was held at Scarborough. The land question, with the organisation of the agricultural worker, was a question very much in the forefront. There were three representatives from the National Union of Agricultural Workers, George was one of the three, the president and the general secretary the other two. The opportunity was given for George to put the union's viewpoint to the congress:

> Your money has been well spent because there has been great success attending these efforts. Thousands of agricultural labourers who had either left their organisation or were disorganised had come into the ranks of the unions catering for agricultural workers. I am very anxious having given fifty-three years out of seventy-five in trying to lead our own people out of the land of bondage into the land of freedom, I say anxious, because in the natural order of things I have soon to lay my weapons down, to see the agricultural labourers so organised that they may take their place in the reorganisation of industry. I am very anxious to see the farm workers take their place side by side with other great organised sections of labour, so hastening on the day and that period in the world's history when serfdom and wage slavery will cease to exist. If that is to take place there must be no two voices coming forward to get them organised. I would again thank the council and the members of congress for their help and generous subscription in trying to organise the agricultural labourer.

It was about this time that the National Council of Agriculture set up a joint committee to put forward an agricultural policy to the government. Labour and trade union representatives were appointed to it, George being one. This committee's report, when presented to the council, showed a recommendation that a subsidy be paid to agriculture of £2 per acre. The committee felt if the system was adopted it should be continued until such a time as a maximum of arable farming promised to become maintainable as an ordinary economic proposition from the improvement of the relation between world prices and the farmers' costs of production. The recommendation was opposed by Mr Walter Smith who had been a president of George's union and was the parliamentary secretary to the ministry of agriculture in the late Labour government. Among the reasons he gave for his opposition was that, in his opinion, the nation must be convinced that it was absolutely necessary before public money was given to support agriculture. Mr Smith said he did not believe that the proposal for a subsidy would necessarily bring a single acre more under the plough.

However, George with his colleagues supported the recommendation. He said that the idea was that the granting of the subsidy would be placed in the hands of agricultural councils or committees who would not give it unless the land was properly cultivated. George went on:

> They (the farmers) could not cultivate land unless they employed labour and if the government took the matter up and granted the subsidy along the lines of the committee's report the first thing that would happen would be that there would be more labour employed on the land, and that is what I'm out for because I am getting alarmed about the depopulation of the villages.

Despite the lengthy and lively debate, this meeting of the National Council of Agriculture accepted the report of its joint committee by a substantial majority. Following the publication of the council's acceptance of the report much argument in the Norfolk press arose from those farmers who believed the recommendation did not meet their needs and because of their advocacy of a system of tariff reform. They had indeed been dissatisfied with the work of the council and critical of George's attitude over barley subsidies. The Norfolk farmers disagreed with farmers in other counties. They had shown their disapproval of George's attitude in March 1924 when, having supported his nomination as president of the council as a direct representative of both sides of the industry, they withdrew from the council. Their action impeded the work and placed George in a very embarrassing position. This action of the farmers upset him to the extent that he looked upon it as a public insult. He was quick to remind them of this when the National Farmers Union officially withdrew from the council with the added excuse that it was unrepresentative in character.

In the press he pointed out that the then president was an ex-chairman of the National Farmers' Union and that other prominent farmers and landowners as well as smallholders were members of the council. He asked with regard to their complaint that the government had not offered the subsidy. 'Well can he (a farmer correspondent) expect that the government will when the Farmers' Union say they will not have it?' Not only from the farmers did George receive criticism concerning the representative nature of the Council of Agriculture and its joint committee but also from Mr George Dallas of the Workers' Union who wrote to Mr Robert Walker, general secretary of the National Union of Agricultural Workers upon the matter. In the letter he wrote: 'I do not know what kind of policy George Edwards will agree to, but no matter what we do, the name of Labour will be associated with any policy he signs his name to, and this may be a very serious thing for the organised workers and the Labour Movements.' He ended his letter by requesting Mr Walker 'to take steps to prevent the name of Labour being attached to any unsound, preposterous or reactionary proposals.' In reply Robert Walker pointed out that George and his colleague, George Hewitt, were not appointed members of the committee as representative of the union. Mr Walker also said he took exception to and resented not only the method, but the manner in which Dallas had approached the matter, emphasising that the National Union of Agricultural Workers was quite capable of taking care of itself as at the same time recognising its responsibilities to the labour movement.

Meanwhile, George, on receiving copies of Dallas's letters, immediately wrote to Mr Walker saying that he was astonished at Mr Dallas's audacity in writing to him on the matter in the spirit he had:

> No one knows better than George Dallas that our union had nothing whatever to do with the setting up of the committee and that I do not sit on the committee as a member of our union, and that I with three others were appointed by the standing committee of the Agricultural Council of which he was a member, and if he did not propose it, he strongly supported it, and it was done at a meeting which I was not present ... I did not know it was passed until you drew my attention to it the morning the council was held, as I had not read the report.

George then went on to add that when the report was moved by the chairman of the committee a resolution moved that the council itself should appoint the committee, which George states he supported, but an amendment had been moved that the report of the committee should be adopted, which Dallas voted for, George voting against it. The amendment, George said, had been carried with an instruction that he and four others should co-opt seven others all who were to be members of the council and that they should draw up a report to be submitted to the next council meeting. After expressing his surprise that Dallas had not informed them that a complaint had been made that no one from The Workers Union had been appointed, he ended his letter by saying, 'Please tell Mr Dallas to attack myself if any one has to be attacked, not our union and I will defend myself. But if a mistake have been made it is he that have made it so far as Labour is concerned and no one else.'

Notes

1. From a newspaper cutting in George's scrapbook dated 11 September 1924. Unfortunately all except the words 'Retford, Worksop, Isle of Axholme' have been cut off from the paper's heading. It is thought to be one of the Winfrey local publications.

2. Taken from George's scrapbook. On the bottom of the pamphlet he wrote lying literature distributed by the Tories in South Norfolk 1924.'

Chapter 10

The Local Arena - Controversies and Contentions

It was during April 1925 that George became involved in a religious controversy in Fakenham with the then Rector, the Revd J.P. Simeon. It arose from an announcement in the *Fakenham Parish Magazine* for that month that the rector would be in the church on Good Friday between 5 and 6.30 to give counsel on spiritual matters and to hear confession. The magazine said that the rector would answer questions respecting this at the next Sunday evening service for which a question box was provided.

George's reaction on reading this was quick. He was planning to preach at the following Sunday morning service at the Fakenham Wesleyan Methodist Church. He took this opportunity to answer the challenge, as he saw it, of the rector to the protestant and to the non-conformist religion. He took as his text 'Did not our hearts burn within us, as he talked with us by the way?' George said that up to the time of that utterance of the text, the disciples of Jesus Christ had absolutely misunderstood his mission. After he had expounded the scriptures they had a totally different vision. Then they came to understand that Christ was not coming to fight the Romans, nor to set up another temporal kingdom, nor to re-establish the old Jewish ritual. They knew that in future their access to God and to the Holiest would be through him (Christ). Upon this they acted and established their church and, according to history, their ritual was of the simplest. As years went by, not being able to throw off their old Judaic religion, they reverted to their former ritual, which in after years became known as Roman Catholicism. Centuries later many of the most learned christians threw off the Roman yoke. Then came the reformation and Martin Luther, with the protestant doctrine. Evidently one section of the christian church never left, Roman Catholicism. They had recent evidence of this in their own town of Fakenham. In the *Fakenham Post* newspaper it was reported that the rector of this parish on the previous Sunday claimed to have power, as a priest of the holy church, as he called it, to hear confessions, and to pronounce absolution and forgiveness, or to retain, where retained, there was no forgiveness. The rector, George said, was also reported as having said that the power was resident in the priesthood, and it made no difference what scurrilous or scandalous life the priest might live, the power was always in the priest, separate altogether from his manhood. 'If that report was true,' George said, 'I myself stand aghast! As a layman of one section of the Protestant Free Churches in the town, I utter the strongest protest against such a romanising teaching in the Church of England. If it came from a Catholic priest, one could say it was honest and sincere, but coming from a minister of the so-called protestant church, which paid protestant money to preach protestant doctrine, all I can say is that it is not honest.' George added that he would challenge the rector to find in the scriptures anything that taught the doctrine of apostolic succession as devolving upon any minister. He considered the time was come when the Free Churches of Fakenham should re-unite, and utter their strongest protests against such a romanising tendency, and romanising utterances by any minister of the protestant church.

As was to be expected, there followed lengthy correspondence in the local press both severely criticising and forcibly supporting George's view and action on this matter. Not only did the rector himself reply in his parish magazine to George's challenge, but the rector of Hempton, the Revd G. Smallpiece, also took up the 'battle' in support of his Fakenham colleague. The substance of which was to endeavour to prove that the rector was acting on the highest authority of the holy church in hearing confessions and in his power as priest to give or not to give absolution for sin. The Fakenham rector said that what the usage's of the Catholic Church had to do with the dissenting sects was beyond comprehension for it was quite certain historically that the Church of England is not protestant but catholic. The rector added that

> On the other hand it must not be forgotten that the church not seldom owes a debt of gratitude to dissenters whose enthusiasm impels them to rush into print in vehement attack. So often the want of knowledge betrayed by these literary efforts breeds in their brethren an uncomfortable sense of insecurity, with the result that they reconsider their position, and enter the church, to become later her devoted and loyal sons. How frequently God works out his purposes in ways unexpected!

Of course George could not let the matter rest there, and once more went onto the attack. This time it was in his own church's pulpit, the Fakenham Primitive Methodist, that he attempted to answer the two rectors and their supporters.

With regard to the question of protestant and catholic definition of the church, George said he had taken all that afternoon to inform himself of the proper definition. In *Nuttall's Standard Dictionary*, which was quite up to date, he found it gave the explanation of the word catholic: 'Universal, embracing, or embraced by the whole Church; liberal; pertaining to, or affecting Roman Catholics, a member of the Roman Catholic Church.' The same dictionary's definition of the word 'Protestant' was: 'One who protests, in the name of the rights of conscience against the authority, in matters spiritual, claimed by the Church of Rome; one of the party who adhered to Luther at the Reformation.' George asked how then could it be said that the Church of England was not a protestant church? He then referred them to history for further proof, instance Wycliffe as a protester against romanism. He ended by saying that it was no use them (the rectors) saying this matter concerned the Church of England alone.

> That, would be right if, like the Catholic Church today, and the Non-conformist bodies, they were supported by voluntary contributions, but the Church of England was supported by compulsory tithes, and thousands of Free Churchmen were compelled to support the Church of England, to whom such Romish teaching was what made their very souls revolt. If a clergyman of the Church of England chose to believe that a priest had the power to give absolution of sins, and that there was such a thing as apostolic succession, he had a perfect right to do so. But, holding such views he should leave the Church, take their courage in his hands and go over to the catholic body.

George added that he made his protest as a humble layman of the protestant church, not as a public man. He was not going to enter into a public controversy in the press. Thus for him the matter ended.

A lighter side of George's activities against exploitation of the working class was noted by the press round about this same period of 1925. He happened to walk down to the market place at Fakenham on Thursday, market-day and stopped to look at a cheap jack who was offering envelopes for sale, one of which was supposed to contain a watch. A schoolboy purchased one and opening the envelope found only a pin with a coloured bead on the end. George demanded the cheap jack to return the boy's money. 'What's it got to do with you?' asked the cheap jack. 'Nothing,' said George, 'Except that I happen to be a magistrate. If you are wise you will return the money and clear out of the town quick.' The advice was accepted without delay.

His concern for the welfare and social improvement of the working people, as in his early days, was still inspired by his interpretation of the Christian gospel. To him the spiritual, moral and social standard of life could not be separated. This conviction had increased with his parliamentary, local government and general public work. It is not surprising therefore that he continued to be active within his church both as a local preacher and active member of its various business meetings. He was a delegate to many of its synods and annual conferences on behalf of his home church and primitive methodist circuit during these years. A local conference of preachers was held at Great Ryburgh Methodist Church, near Fakenham. George had been invited to give a paper on 'The History and Place of Lay Preaching.' This aroused a lively discussion on methods to adopt to bring men and women, and particularly young people, to God and active church membership. It was emphasised that the numbers of young people entering the church and offering themselves for the work of lay preaching continued to decrease. Some of the older preachers present were strong in their denunciation of the activities of young people in their love for whist drives, socials and dances. They deplored the loss of the old-time prayer meetings and bible classes.

In replying to the debate George observed that their forefathers had a different type of man to appeal to,

> by appealing to his animal nature, they were able to do some wonderful work. Today they had a different type to deal with, while science and research had developed, the good old truth remained the same, but presented itself to us in a different way. We have to show men that religion stood for something noble and good. Our young people were asking what religion has to offer. What part are we going to take to show them that religion had something better upon which to build up the world than materialism?

He then urged the conference to go on with their old truths by all means, but to adapt themselves to convey it forcibly, clearly and intelligently. If they did that, he had no fear for organised christianity.

Once more, following the highlighting in the press of George's address, he found himself assailed both by press and personal correspondence for his political and union activities, particularly for his continued support of Sunday union demonstrations. It was inferred that he was partly to blame for the 'different type they had to deal with' and the decline in church membership with the over-emphasis upon materialism. But this criticism, even though some came from his own church members and some of his fellow lay preachers, did not cause him the distress that such criticism had done in the past, and he pressed on regardless with his religious work.

The move towards Methodist union was gaining momentum and George found himself actively supporting it. He received invitations to give lectures upon the subject and that of the history of Methodism. Elm, near Wisbech, was one of the places to which he was invited to conduct special services and to give such a lecture. The following extract from this particular lecture shows how he felt the urgency of the need for the church to be more actively concerned with everyday problems that arose from the moral and social life of the people and nation. He tried to emphasise in his lecture that both the Christ they professed to worship and the founder of their church, John Wesley, had been concerned and involved with these issues of everyday life.

What is to be our future? We are not yet played nor have we finished our work. We have got to grapple with the materialistic tendency of the age. Further we have got to face the fact we have not reached a finality of human progress. Every advancement in this direction only makes the unsolved problems look in more acute form. With the advancement of democratic thought of which [we the church] have done our bit to mould. The great bulk of our countrymen have different outlooks on life and are pressing forward for an entire reconstruction of our national life, they have lofty ideals. Now what is going to be our action in reference to these great ideals. I want to say quite frankly that if we as a church adopt a principle of standing aloof or what would be worse would be an attitude of hostility, then I have great fear of the future. I don't mean that as a church we are to become embroiled in political warfare. What I do mean is we must endeavour to infuse in all these great problems a spiritual atmosphere and do our part to see that this new kingdom which is bound to come is laid with such righteous materials as Christ embodied in all teaching as recorded in the bible. Oh! For the sake of our old religious principle and the cause of religious freedom for which the founder of our great Methodist Churches fought and suffered so much to obtain for us don't let us stand aloof. We see by history what disastrous moral results, spiritually the indifference of the Churches had upon our national life in these days that are past. Let us take warning and prevent such catastrophe happening in the future. Let us each and all work for a great spiritual revival in every department of our national life and no church is better equipped than our own. And may I appeal to you my brethren who up to present have not been able to go with some of us in our public movements and perhaps because you have not been quite able to understand us have been rather disposed to condemn us some time, do not lay a stone in our path. But rather hold out the hand of sympathy. We have our domestic troubles. We are doing our best, some with difficulties, to keep high in the great industrial and national life the great spiritual ideals and to keep the movement in the path of moderation and sweet reasonableness and to bring about the kingdom of equality and justice by evolution and not by revolution.

George also received many invitations from various churches, religious and other organisations to relate his life story. This proved popular both inside his own locality and even outside the county. Especially so within his own church organisation for he used to use the old hymns and their tunes, some of which he himself sang as a solo, to illustrate his early preaching days. Also the story was always made more humorous by his impersonation of some of the old 'hell-fire' preachers' methods of warning of the coming damnation to unrepentant sinners. He would tell of their mode of expression and the way they illustrated their texts.

One such was of the local preacher whose sermon was based upon the story of Daniel in the lion's den. This particular preacher was very forceful in his method of illustration of Daniel's deliverance. He would shout, 'Where art thou, oh! Daniel,' and then descending from the pulpit, having thrown his jacket down, he would walk among the congregation and raise his hands above his head, shouting 'Here, O Lord, among the lions.' George said this did not amuse his congregation, but more often offended them. Telling further of his religious experiences of his early days, he emphasised the faith and deep-rooted belief in the power of prayer of the local preachers and class leaders, George said they would be often carried away by their fervour and emotion. This would lead them to express themselves crudely and in strange phrases. He told of one sincere and aged preacher, a leader, who on one occasion prayed, 'Oh Lord, send down Thy stars like a bunch of grapes. Come down among us, come through the roof, I'll pay for it to be mended.' Then there was the young local preacher whom George remembered was very conscious of the presence amongst his congregation of those who were to judge his ability to be accepted as a fully accredited local preacher. He took for his text, 'Ye are spies to see the nakedness of the land ye are come' (Gen. 42 V 9).

These lecture tours often meant travelling many miles from home to little villages which the railway did not serve. Mr Ernest Powell, a member of the well-known local Fakenham harness-making family, who were prominent and active in the Primitive Methodist Church, had by this time acquired a Ford motor car (then known as the 'Tin-Lizzie'). For a small charge he took George to most of his meetings. The hire-charge for those organised by the Agricultural Workers Union, of course, were paid for by them. Before the car was acquired the Powell family kindly loaned one or two pony carts for the use of the church's preachers that had to conduct services in the villages and also to convey George and some of his colleagues to union meetings. A wagon was also loaned for use as a platform for the outdoor meetings in Fakenham. On one occasion a large pony cart was used to carry three or four people to a meeting. The cart had a small door at the rear for the passengers to get in. On this particular occasion one of the passengers, who was rather fat, in endeavouring to get into the cart got set fast in the doorway. It took all the power of the rest to push and pull before the unfortunate passenger managed to get inside the cart. Alighting from it was equally a hazardous task, but this time his colleagues managed to lift him over the side without any harm to him.

The many speaking arrangements George had he never took a penny for his services, simply charging for his travelling expenses and lodging when it necessitated his spending the night away from home. This refusal to charge for his services was not because his personal financial position had improved as a result of his parliamentary work. In fact quite the opposite was the true position. The Parliamentary salary of £600 per annum, might to many in those days have appeared a lot, but it did not leave him much for himself, after paying his London lodgings, postage, train, bus and tube charges and the rent and upkeep of his Fakenham home and providing for his house-keeper and adopted son. Added to this were the many appeals (with which public men are inundated) for various charitable causes, as well as that of his church. Whilst it was, of course, impossible to assist all that he would have liked, many he did. His salary, after his defeat at the general election, as a part-time union organiser was insufficient by itself. But due to the generosity of his two good friends, Herbert Day and Noel Buxton, he was often saved from real financial embarrassment.

Unfortunately, not all realised what his self-sacrificing public work had meant to him. Some misguided people who had got themselves into difficult situations not only expected him to give them the benefit of his advice but also expected monetary help as well. Many were the pitiful stories some of them told him, and often he drew upon his small personal savings to assist them. But the time soon came when this had to stop. He was not prepared to allow his own friends to provide him with monetary aid only to give it away to those desiring to take advantage of his sympathetic and tender-heartedness by sponging upon him. When this happened and he refused to aid such people, he was violently abused, abuse which sometimes was veiled with threats to his person. Some of this abuse came from a few people for whom he had done much and shown much care and concern, and who should have known better.

He was always particularly interested in work for young people, and always tried to see their viewpoint. Misunderstanding of him by some did not in any way alter his affection or concern for them. Sometimes when they criticised him because they felt his methods were old-fashioned or too slow for them and would be too long in achieving the reforms they shared with him in desiring, he would laugh and tell them, 'You are young men in a hurry, the years of experience will show you some of the methods you desire not to employ will have had the opposite effect.' George believed in the proverb that is was wisest to 'Make haste slowly.' So he tried to remain always patient with the young and all who differed from him.

Whilst George's political and union activities often took him from his home town and county, his resolve to concentrate more effort on behalf of the workers through the medium of the local government channels after his electoral defeat at the parliamentary general election, was not affected or forgotten. He increased his activities upon the county, district and parish councils. To assist in getting a better picture of these activities and the varied challenges he faced, it will be necessary to take a retrospective glance.

It had been in 1919 that he was first elected to the Fakenham parish council, of which he remained chairman until 1922. He then resigned from that body at the triennial election due to the pressure of other public duties. It should be noted that in those days parish councillors were elected at the annual parish meeting of electors, every three years, by a show of hands unless five electors demanded a poll after the result of the show of hands had been declared. During his first three-year period of office as parish councillor, George advocated and gave support to the move to acquire a new recreation ground. That in use was situated some distance from the town's centre, by the side of the river Wensum near to Dewing and Kerseley's flour mill and by the side of the Fakenham Gas Works.[1] There was a dyke running by its side which took the waste tar substance from the gas works. The ground itself was very damp and far from ideal for recreational purposes. Among other amenities which George felt were needed in the town and to which he lent his support were a public convenience, additional allotments and a bathing place. His union made a loan towards the purchase of additional allotments, and these were eventually acquired. But the other amenities were not, and became prominent issues of controversy for many years.

At the annual parish meeting of 1925, which was again the occasion of the triennial elections of parish councillors, George attended. Although not standing for election, he asked some searching questions of those who were, among which were: (i) Are the candidates in favour of a recreation ground for the town of Fakenham? (ii) Will they consider the question of a public convenience for the town? (iii) Are they in favour of a public swimming bath for the town?

However, it soon became evident that the newly elected councillors, comprising mostly business people, were opposed to the provision of these amenities. Their view was that the result would be a heavy burden upon the rates. Delaying tactics were thus continually used by them in the form of reference of these issues to various bodies such as the Charity

Commissioners and Norfolk County Council to see if a way could be found to acquiring these amenities, without the cost falling on the rates and if possible to obtain some help from these bodies.

George, himself, had long thought the town should acquire urban status. It was his view that if such was the case more progress could be made in the town and at least some of the much needed amenities might be more easily acquired. No doubt with this in mind, he asked at the annual parish meeting of 1926 whether the parish council had recently considered the question of urban powers for the parish of Fakenham. The reply he received was 'Yes! But the Council did not feel any advantage would be gained for the extra cost entailed, probably the only advantage would be they would be their own masters.'

His efforts as a member of the Walsingham Rural District Council were mainly in the sphere of the Board of Guardians (assisting those needing public assistance), the Employment Committee (of which for its short duration he was vice-chairman), and the Housing Committee. In October 1923, speaking on the general housing problem of the district, he said he deprecated giving assistance to private owners to build, and urged the council not to part with any of its unused building land to private owners. 'I am of the opinion,' he said 'that the Council should itself undertake further building operations to meet the need for additional housing accommodation, and am of the opinion that with the rents obtainable and the government assistance offered this could be down without the rates being burdened with resultant loss.' This was another form his efforts took to overcome the vexed question of the farm tied-cottage which continued to threaten most of the members of his union who were numbered among the many people who could ill afford to buy their own houses or find other rented property they could meet the expense of.

The Rating and Valuation Act of 1925 George saw would give further assistance to the farming community, which should enable the employers to pay better wages and offer improved working conditions, assisting thereby in a peaceful revolution in the countryside.[2] Perhaps this was in his mind as he told the Board of Guardians meeting: 'What wonderful times we are living in. I hope the word revolution will never more form a bugbear, for if the rating alteration did not constitute a revolution of our system, I do not know what would.' Referring to the clause providing for agricultural land and buildings being rated on a quarter the actual value, he recalled that he understood the Chancellor of the Exchequer to make it clear that while government assistance in the form of a grant would be continued in the case of the rating of agricultural land, it would not be given to make up the decreased rates that would be paid on agricultural buildings.

During October 1925, an election took place in Fakenham to fill a vacancy on the Walsingham RDC. Some months previously George was approached by a farmer friend on the Norfolk County Council, whose wife happened to be a leading local Tory, who inquired whether, if a vacancy on the Walsingham RDC for Fakenham arose, he, George, would be willing to stand for it and give up his seat which he held at the little village of Pensthorpe. This would allow Mr W.E. Porter, another farmer living there, to become the member for his own village. George understood from his Conservative friend that if he agreed to this that he would not be opposed at Fakenham because this was what the local Tories desired. He accepted this in good faith and agreed to the arrangement. But when nomination day came he found himself opposed by an official Tory candidate and he was defeated. Salt was rubbed into the wound of defeat by the fact that the wife of the person who had made the suggestion had openly canvassed against him, making play on the fact that George was already a member of the RDC for Pensthorpe.

It would seem that on this occasion, as on that of his differences with the farmers over the representation on the Council of Agriculture, that he was inclined to mistake the wide and sincere respect he had acquired from his opponents as a guarantee of support which would on all occasions override deep-rooted political affiliations. When this did not happen, he was deeply hurt and took personal umbrage. Yet he did not harbour a grievance against any who he felt had deceived him, but tried therein to differentiate between trusting a person as a person and trusting them politically.

Notes

1. Still known as the Old Recreation Ground and administered by the Town Council. Some light industries are sited there as well as a picnic area, park and skateboard facility.

2. A 75 per cent reduction in general rates was given by the Agricultural Rates Acts 1896 and 1923. Full reduction of rates on agricultural buildings was given under Section 67 of the Local Government Act, 1929.

Chapter 11

The General Strike and other Battles

The year 1926 began with industrial unrest seething throughout the whole country as a result of unemployment and low wages and the accompanying high cost of living. In Norfolk the Norfolk Agricultural Wages Committee turned down the union's demand for wages to be increased from twenty eight to thirty five shillings per week. The men were greatly incensed by this and the union called a conference of its Norfolk members to consider what action should now be taken. A resolution was passed, after much discussion in which very strong feelings were expressed, affirming continued confidence in, and appreciation for, what their leaders had done in their endeavour to improve the lot of the land worker. It instructed their national executive to take the matter in hand and open up negotiations with the government, failing a satisfactory solution they were to take whatever further action they deemed proper. The resolution pledged the conference's wholehearted support in any action that they might decide to take.

The union's representative followed this conference's instruction and made representation to the minister of agriculture, asking him to use the power the Agriculture Act gave him to request the chairman of the Norfolk Wages Committee to call another meeting to reconsider its refusal to grant the wage increase. But the minister refused to do this or to intervene in the matter. Therefore the executive committee immediately called every one of its Norfolk union branches to hold a special meeting and urge every member to attend. Ballot papers were supplied to enable the members to vote in secret for or against strike action. The votes would be counted later in the union headquarters at London. George and other executive members were instructed to attend these special branch meetings to advise the members upon the action that had been taken on their behalf and on matters of procedure with regard to the ballot and the counting of the votes, but they themselves were not to endeavour to persuade the members either one way or the other on the way to vote, neither were they to vote themselves. This was to ensure that the action ultimately decided on should be completely the will of the members.

George was filled with foreboding over the situation. He did not want to see a repetition of the Norfolk strike of 1923 with all its resulting bitterness.

He was severely criticised by the farming community for his continued advocacy of higher wages for the farm workers at a time when they said they could ill afford to pay more. He answered these criticisms both through the columns of the local press and at meetings of the workers. He said the workers had right on their side, there had been no demand made on their behalf which was not just, fair or reasonable. Every time they asked for anything they were met by the pleas 'We cannot afford it.' George said,

> I do not accept it - on whom did the blame rest? The fault is not with the agricultural labourers. They were honest and skilful and as good workers as any to be found in any county in England. Sometimes my blood boils when I hear how farmers talk about the men. They say they do not mind paying good wages to good men, but did not like paying them to ordinary men. I would like to know where the good men were according to the farmers. But the present position was not all the farmers' fault. Some fault rested with the men who were not in the Union. If the workers' representatives had gone to the District Wages Committee and said they were speaking for 95 per cent of the agricultural workers there would have been no deadlock.

Meanwhile the unrest in other parts of the country was quickly coming to a head, and the General Strike that eventually ensued was sparked off from the dispute in the coal-mining industry. The coal owners posted notices to the effect that the pits would be open on terms which the men refused to accept. Thus the miners were locked-out. The general unrest throughout industry led to the TUC giving support to the miners by way of a General Strike, which of course involved the agricultural workers. But before this eventually happened, bands of miners visited Norfolk seeking support for their cause. George found himself criticised by some of the farm workers for his efforts to raise money for the miners when they were also in difficulties, but he disregarded this and continued to do all he could to promote the welfare of all workers, as he said, they should all stand together and help one another if victory was ever to be achieved.

During this period a band of two dozen miners from Doncaster arrived in Fakenham quite unexpectedly. They called upon George for advice and assistance. They were travelling the countryside with mouth organs, cornets, accordions and improvised instruments such as combs and tissue paper, playing various popular songs while they marched, and held meetings to promote their cause and gain support for their wives and families. At such notice George found it difficult to find them accommodation, but managed to borrow blankets and mattresses which he put down in his bedrooms, giving up his own bed for them, and sleeping on a couch himself. A kind friend, and fellow methodist, who owned a local temperance hotel, offered to assist with feeding the men which considerably eased the situation for George. The town band also generously answered George's pleas for help for the miners by playing in the evening in the market square and giving their collection to the miners. George also arranged for the miners to visit Cromer where his friend Mr Noel Buxton and his agent obtained permission for them to parade and play on the promenade and in the streets whilst collecting for their funds. Later, on their return to Fakenham, a public meeting, which George had organised, was held in the Square at which their leaders with other local trade unionists, and George spoke in support of the miners' cause, and a collection was taken up.

Upon another occasion a Welsh miners' prize choir from Newbridge visited the town. George was able to gain much sympathy for them from his friends at the Primitive Methodist Church. They were invited to sing at a special service there, after which they gave a sacred concert in the old Corn Hall. Both the service and the concert were well attended. The collections were given to the miners' funds. Before the choir left the town they gathered on the local railway station platform where George had gone to see them off, and as a farewell tribute and appreciation for his efforts on their behalf they gave a wonderful rendering of the tune 'Diadem'.

One day a lone miner called at George's home, saying he was from Doncaster. He told a most moving story of the poverty of his wife and children and how he endeavoured to find alternative work in his own home town and county without success. So he said he had looked further afield. He had tramped on foot, stopping at various places en route to do odd jobs for people and enlist support for his family and comrades in similar distress. The heart-rending story he told touched George's heart. Not only did he offer him board and lodgings, he obtained fresh clothes for him and a temporary job at a local builders. Friends loaned him tools and gave money for him to send home to his wife. The man continued to do odd jobs in the town for two or three weeks, but disappeared one day and was never seen again. Apparently he had got what he wanted and then absconded. It was later learned through inquiries that were made that this particular man had worked this kind of confidence trick in other areas. As a result of this experience it became more difficult for George to get and maintain support from friends and the town's people for others in need who were genuine. But this was a rare case in the many that he assisted during this period.

With the advent of the General Strike, George assisted in the forming of a local strike committee comprising representatives of all the local trade unions, railwaymen, printers, building workers and his own agricultural workers. The largest numbers of those involved locally in the strike were those employed at the local printing works. George was appointed chairman of the strike committee whose job was to organise concerts and demonstrations to enlist public support and raise money to implement the meagre strike pay many of them were able to obtain from their respective unions. He also found himself called upon to keep the men united in their stand. In reporting the situation to his own union general secretary he says that whilst the railwaymen remained, 'Solid to a man, whatever may be said to the contrary' he found some dissatisfaction amongst the printers over the question of strike pay and some tendency to return to work. He wrote,

> I met them again today as I have every day and used all my persuasive powers to keep them out, but I am afraid, however, unless something more reassuring can be given them within a few hours most of the printers will be back which will have a bad moral effect on the rest.

Help by way of money did arrive soon after and the situation was saved. He had managed to obtain the loan of the local Labour Party Rooms[1] for the strikers, particularly the printers, to use during the day and evening for meetings and recreation.

Despite the many disappointments and much opposition, he pressed on in his efforts to assist those in need and to promote the well-being of the working classes without thought for himself. One of the avenues through which he directed his efforts to this end was the Walsingham Rural District Council's Employment Committee and that of the Fuel and General Emergency Committee of which he was a member. This latter committee had been set up to deal with any matters of urgency arising during the strike which might affect the welfare or cause personal hardship to the district's population through possible shortage of food supplies, etc. The strain of these efforts, and the constant battling against the odds of misinterpretation of his motives (for he was still branded by many as an agitator and strike-maker), seriously affected his health. He collapsed one day when attending a meeting. The doctor ordered him to bed as his condition was serious, diagnosing dropsy with a further weakening to the heart.

Great concern was felt for him as the weeks went by. The doctor doubted very much whether George would ever get downstairs again. He warned him that only a complete rest and quietude could bring him round. But George always knew when anyone came to the house to see him, no matter what precautions were taken to keep him undisturbed. He worried in case anyone should be turned away who really needed his help. It became better policy to let him see them, if only for a few minutes. As his strength gradually returned he was allowed to sit up in bed and to write his monthly articles for his union's magazine, *The Landworker*. In these articles he called upon the land workers to remain firm in their just demands and to be loyal to the union. He now accepted that his life's work was almost over, having taken note of his doctor's advice regarding his heart. It was in light of this condition that he wrote:

> And now what of the future? Let me say to my younger brethren, upon whose shoulders will fall the burden of the coming struggle your work is only just begun. There are many problems that have yet to be solved, and when these are settled others will arise equally important. My day is declining, and I feel the time has come when I shall have to lay the weapons of warfare down. But whatever is done the union must not die. The forces that will be arrayed against it will be powerful and strong, and will require united efforts to defeat them. But with calm thoughts and sound judgement the land of prosperity and freedom will be reached. In the hour of my sad affliction and weakness I conclude:
>
> > Courage then my brother,
> > The day has come at last
> > The clouds are lifting quickly,
> > The night is breaking fast;
> > Be strong then, and take courage,
> > Our cause is just and right
> > And he who holds by justice
> > Is sure to win the fight.

However, through the same courage and will power within himself that he had urged upon his comrades, eventually he was enabled to make a slow, but sure recovery, to the joy and amazement of those nearest to him. But for quite a time he had to be taken about in a bath-chair. This was the hardest part for him to bear. He felt so much better in himself and could not bear to be so dependant upon others, especially when there appeared so much that he felt he ought and could do. At this time the farm workers' wages was thirty shillings per week which the farmers were loud in their lamentations that they could not afford to pay. Many men were being paid off, especially the older men, whilst at the same time Irish labour was being used upon some farms. The tied cottage problem was still increasingly worrying to those employed on the farms lest they should be faced with eviction upon being paid off by their employers. How then, thought George, could he be expected to take things quietly and rest? He felt he should now be assisting his union colleagues to tackle these problems on behalf of the men.

He was eventually able to take up active public work in 1928, but his doctor emphasised that he must be sure and not over-tax his heart. He must continue to go slowly and carefully and not take risks. We see him renewing his efforts in 1928 on behalf of the workers as a member of the Walsingham Rural District Council. The rural district council at the time was responsible for some of the men who had had to leave farmwork and been able to obtain work as roadmen and on various maintenance work.

In February, 1928, George supported a resolution at the R.D.C. meeting:

(a) that all workmen employed by this Council on reaching the age of 65 years shall continue to be paid the full rate of wages providing they are able to do a full day's work each day as required.

(b) That any workman employed by this Council who is unable to do a full day's work each day as required shall have his disability assessed by the Highways Committee and shall be paid wages in accordance with that assessment, but any workman being dissatisfied with the Highways Committee's decision shall appear before the Council who shall review the assessment and revise it if necessary.

This resolution was carried. George then moved the following resolution:

That having regard to the fact that the Widows, Orphans and Old Age (Contributions) Pension Act has deprived all insured persons of 65 years and over of their cash benefits under the National Health Insurance Act, all regularly employed workmen of the Council of 65 years of age or over who fall sick and is unable to work, shall receive full wages, less ten shillings per week from the Council for a period not exceeding six weeks. A doctor's certificate of unfitness for work must be submitted to the Clerk to the Council each week before payment is made.

He lost this resolution by a majority of 16.

Mindful of the doctor's instruction to avoid taking risks with his health, George felt he could do this by concentrating his main efforts within his own parish and district for a time. Thus having so well recovered his strength he decided to accept the invitation of his local friends to stand again for the Fakenham parish council. The election that year (1928) was held on 12 March and on this occasion George was elected for his final term of office on this council.

There had long been an agitation in Fakenham for the provision of bathing facilities and a new playing field for the parish's children, and George, as we saw, was in favour of both amenities being provided. With regard to the issue of the playing field, he shared the view of many of the townsmen that the old recreation ground was totally unsuited for that purpose. It was also some distance from the local school and residential area. The issue was highlighted in the local press which became the medium for the debate that followed.

As in the past over such controversies, George was soon drawn into it. The issue cut right across the normal political boundaries and he found himself opposed by some of his Labour party friends who took the view that Hempton Green, about a mile from Fakenham in the adjoining parish of Hempton, and free for all to use, was adequate for the need. They further declared that if the old recreation ground were to be given proper attention, the children's recreational needs would be well catered for. They considered it would be folly to spend the ratepayers' money for provision of a new playing field when there were prior needs such as a proper sewerage scheme and a local hospital. They emphasised that the local rate was already too high. In attacking these views, George pointed out that Hempton Green was not in the parish of Fakenham, that a large proportion of it was used by football and cricket clubs, and to get to it the Fakenham children would have to go by the river or through the most dangerous street in town. With regard to the existing recreation ground he said, 'It is well known that, spend what money you may on this field, it is impossible to make it fit for children to play on. A great part of it is below the bed of the river, and a filthy old open drain runs by the side of it, full of old dirty gas muck from the gas works.' He then challenged his opponents of the new playing field to point to one open space in the town where children could play. He said, 'We have 200 houses in Fakenham with no back yard, with no space for children to play in but the street.' Turning to the question of the rates he continued,

> It [the new playing field] need not cost the ratepayers of the town more than a fraction of a penny in the pound to purchase the field offered and prepare it for the children to play on. The Council has already £350 in hand, the money paid for the piece of the old recreation ground sold some years ago, which they cannot spend for any other purpose other than the purchase of land for the public use. They also have an income of £10 per year for the old piece of a field which must be saved as they can spend it for no other purpose.

Having once more become a member of the Fakenham parish council, he was able to join forces with those councillors who had been active in their support for a new playing field. It was thought that a site adjoining the Queen's Road School (opposite to where George was then living) was a good proposition, and might be available. However, a resolution to enter into negotiation with the owners was defeated by one vote. George supported a resolution for the question to be resolved by a poll. This was carried. The town's electors were called upon to vote at a poll of 26 March 1928, on the following resolution:

> That the Fakenham elector's instruct the Fakenham Parish Council at its first regular held meeting to take steps to utilise the money now in the Recreation Ground Account, and any other available moneys, such as that from the Old Recreation Ground and rent of the School Gardens, to purchase ground belonging to Caius College, Cambridge, and adjoining the schools as a playing field so as to be available for the children of Fakenham.

The result of the poll was: For the Resolution   255

Against the Resolution   259

Thus the move to acquire a new playing field was defeated by only four votes.

Despite the result of the poll, George and his friends on the parish council did not let the matter drop. They made another move to re-open the question in May of that year, but once more the opponents of the venture defeated them. Nevertheless the fight both for the playing field and for swimming facilities continued year in year out, with George's active support which continued after his final defeat at the next triennial parish council elections of 1931. He was elected at this particular election by a show of hands, but a poll was demanded and he was defeated.

With continued improvement in health and strength George gradually extended again his activities beyond his home town and, indeed, county. In May 1928 he was able to attend the biennial conference of his union. The main topic at this conference was the unrest in the agricultural industry. In the debate George spoke on the question of the tied cottage and then moved a resolution that

> This conference declares that any agricultural policy satisfactory to the farm workers must include in its proposals: the total abolition of the tied cottage; the restoration of full powers to the Central Wages Board; a special scheme of unemployment insurance for agricultural workers; payment of representatives appointed to the county agricultural committee; a scheme of land nationalisation and provisions that land shall be held conditionally upon the occupier cultivating it in accordance with recognised standards of good husbandry.

He concluded his speech with words that showed renewed hope and determination to carry on the fight for the farm workers for some time to come.

> I would like to take the opportunity of expressing the gratitude for the kind expressions I have received in regard to my health. I hope, with our

chairman, that this may not be the last time by any means that I shall meet you. I hope I may live to see the great organisation which was started in 1906, covering the length and breadth of this land, with not an agricultural labourer outside its ranks. If I live to see that, then at least I shall know that the English labourer is free.

On 3 June 1928 a great Norfolk demonstration of the Agricultural Workers Union was held at Hempton Green, Fakenham. Before marching to the green, headed by a silver band, George unfurled in Fakenham market place a new county banner. At the demonstration he was one of the chief speakers. He urged the land workers to continue to work to enrol all their fellow workers within the ranks of the union and to carry on the fight for improved conditions and security.

His activities within his own home district continued mainly on the Walsingham RDC and the Fakenham magistrates bench. His work upon the rural district council shows his outlook was not narrow nor confined to the welfare of the farm workers alone, but that he recognised his responsibilities to the whole community which it was always his sincere desire to serve. He knew that the welfare of his own class depended upon the general welfare being maintained of the community as a whole. Often he was suspicious that certain moves of councillors were directed to serving private interests, although veiled under a cloak of so-called protection of the rate payer. Also he was certain within himself that many measures advocated for economy reasons would in the long run prove false economy.

The rural district council had at this time had the responsibility of administering a children's home situated at The Red House, Little Snoring, about three miles from Fakenham. He supported vigorously efforts to get conditions there improved. It meant the council spending money, and although some opposed the spending of money upon it, it was eventually agreed this should be done. At this time also there was a move to acquire better premises for meetings of the council and office accommodation. The council had for long been meeting at Thursford Workhouse, which was about five miles from Fakenham, not a very convenient or satisfactory place either to get to or hold meetings, particularly as its chief officers had to do their work in private offices in Fakenham. When premises were found in Bridge Street, Fakenham, which the clerk of the council thought suitable for its purposes, the council agreed to enter into agreement to purchase it. But some councillors tried to get the council at its next meeting to scrap the agreement and to purchase land to build new offices upon or, alternatively, to use rooms in another private building in the town.

George was very concerned that such a move should be made. It was to him false economy and he intuitively felt there was more behind the move than appeared on the surface. But of this he had no proof and therefore did not voice these sentiments publicly. The mover of a resolution that would have had the effect of scrapping the agreement to purchase or if this was too late to resell the Bridge Street premises and acquire alternative premises, gave as his reasons. 'On grounds of agriculture depression it was unwise to spend money at such a time.' He added, 'This applied also to money spent on the children's home,' which he considered unwise for the same reason. Replying to this George said, 'The resolution was very belated and I am surprised that the arguments raised had not been raised earlier.' He then asked for information as to the property suggested as an alternative and said that 'if it was thought of buying land and buildings, that when a playing field was required in Fakenham, something like £110 per acre was asked for land,' and so 'the council will be wise in the circumstances to carry out the agreement it has entered into and complete the purchase.' This was eventually agreed upon a majority vote.

His activities of 1928 show what a remarkable recovery in health and strength he had made. Active both in mind and body, he had been enabled to tackle with vigour the many every day problems that faced the community at that time. He was now seventy-eight, but the only visible sign of his age physically was that his hearing had become impaired. An amusing incident occurred one day as a result of this. He was walking home from the town with his housekeeper when they chanced to meet a lady who attended their church but had not been able to do so for some time having had what was thought to be lumbago. His housekeeper told George this just before they met up with the lady. To her embarrassment, George, stopping to speak to the good lady inquired, 'And how is the new baby?'

Notes

1.   Later the Town Band Room, now Jehovah's Witness Temple.

Chapter 12

Knighthood

It became evident early in 1929 that a general election was imminent. The Tory government had been in office nearly its full term of five years. George's health had now so improved that he really felt himself to be more his old warring self again. He was eager to enter the electoral fight on behalf of his Labour colleagues. He soon began to help in the preparation to do battle on their behalf in Norfolk, particularly for his old friends, Noel Buxton and W.B. Taylor. Noel Buxton was defending his seat in North Norfolk and W.B. Taylor was standing for South-West Norfolk. Indeed, had George been the candidate he could not have spoken at more meetings, nor could his enthusiasm have been greater.

His efforts were rewarded; his two colleagues were elected. But his delight was even greater when he learnt the result nationally was the return of a Labour government. True, the fact that it was again to be a minority government without an overall majority over the other parties, did rather take the 'gilt off the gingerbread' for him. But in common with most of his colleagues and trade union leaders, he believed that Ramsay MacDonald would counteract the Tory majority of the Lords by creating sufficient Labour peers, to prevent them defeating the government by throwing out important legislation.

The Labour candidate for South Norfolk (George's late constituency) Mr George Young, probably had this thought in mind as a possible action by MacDonald should he be called upon again to head a minority government. He made an unfortunate statement at a public meeting which gave the impression that George would be one of the new peers. After the election this impression had gained ground, and seemed to have become taken for granted even by some of George's closest colleagues. He himself was led to believe this might be so. When he met his friend W.B. Taylor at Norwich soon after the election, he drew Mr Taylor's attention to Mr Young's statement which had appeared in the press. He inquired of him whether he had heard any confirmation of it. 'WB' (as he was known to his friends) told George he had heard that the prime minister would invite him to accept a knighthood, but suggested that he, George, should write to him, 'WB', about it so that he could present the copy of the letter to those concerned in the matter within the parliamentary Labour party. George followed his advice and wrote:

> Referring to our conversation at Norwich on Saturday last, re the peerage. As you are already aware the action in reference to same was taken by Mr George Young, late Labour candidate for South Norfolk, without my knowledge or consent, and he made a public statement. He spoke with authority, that if the Labour Party were returned to power the first thing they would do would be to make me a peer. Coming from such a quarter the public accepted it as a fact, and expected it, and when it did not materialise our own friends, and the public generally were disappointed. I have already informed you I am not personally anxious about it, but I am extremely anxious about it on behalf of our friends, and my fellow workers.

George then added that if the peerage were conferred upon him it would be seen to 'be opening the door of all our parliamentary institutions to every class of the community.' With regard to the alternative honour of a knighthood, George gave it as his opinion that it was not so desirable to his people as that of the peerage for by a peerage he would be in a better position to do more useful work in his latter days on their behalf. Whilst, as his letter to his friend 'WB' implied, he desired to remain in a humble position, the fact remained that Mr Young's statement caused him much personal embarrassment. It worried him in case the agricultural workers should believe that they had been let down. However, this feeling was quickly dispelled and he became convinced that no real harm was done to them when he saw how thrilled they were when the news eventually came to them that their George had been granted a knighthood in the King's birthday honours list. In retrospect, he fully accepted that the knighthood had served the same desired end of recognition of the land worker as a peerage.

It was on 21 May 1930, that he received the official intimation from the Prime Minister's secretary which said that it was the prime minister's 'intention in respect of the forthcoming list of birthday honours to submit your name to the King with a recommendation that he may be graciously pleased to approve that the honour of Knighthood be conferred upon you.' To which he replied, 'Please thank the Prime Minister for me, for his thoughtfulness in offering to submit my name to the King, to confer on me the honour of Knighthood. Kindly assure the Prime Minister that should the King be graciously pleased to accept his recommendation I shall have the greatest pleasure in accepting.'

The final list of those receiving birthday honours showed George's name among those receiving the knighthood. The words appended to it were: 'For services to agricultural workers'. And that was the way in which George himself looked upon it. The news was greeted throughout the country, particularly in Norfolk, with enthusiastic approval. The day of his investiture arrived, 13 June 1930. It brought back to him the memory of the previous occasion when he was invested with the OBE. As on that occasion, so now he felt a little nervous. Miss Myers, his housekeeper, accompanied him to London. He withstood the journey and the excitement of the ceremony well, considering his eighty years and a weakened heart. On arriving at Buckingham Palace he found that as he was to be a knight bachelor he was to be the first to see the King. Following the ceremony he attended a special executive meeting of his union at their head office. There he was greeted with loud applause upon entering the room. They passed a resolution before he left for home which congratulated him upon the honour conferred upon him and recorded the appreciation the executive had for his life long efforts on behalf of the agricultural worker.

6. *Sir George Edwards and the author at Fakenham, 1930.*

George and Miss Myers left London about 3 pm. When they arrived at Fakenham they were met by the author of this book and a great public reception, headed by the Fakenham town band, local councillors, trade union and labour party officials, clergy and British Legion representatives. A great procession followed the car which took him to Fakenham Market Place. There hundreds more thronged around him singing 'For he's a jolly good fellow.' Flags and bunting were hung from the windows of the shops and business premises of the town. A platform had been erected in the market square to which he was escorted. Speeches of congratulation and welcome were then made by the chairman of the Fakenham Parish Council, Mr E. Long and others. Following these George was presented with an aid-to-deafness battery set, collected for by numerous friends and organisations as a token of respect and appreciation of his public work. In receiving this gift, George, filled with emotion, said that the occasion was a happy sign to him that, though people might differ vitally on important matters in public life, that fact did not prevent good feeling from prevailing among them. He added,

> This great honour now conferred upon me I do not hold merely as a personal honour, but a recognition of the importance the agricultural labourer is to the state, and I hope both they and my own beloved Church for whom I have lived and worked will look upon it as an honour conferred upon them. My name is altered, but I am not. It is not the purse or the honour that makes a man, but his character and the work he does. My only object has been to raise up the class in which I was born in dire poverty. I am proud that in my lifetime I have witnessed such changes as I have. We older men have laid the foundations of the new society. On them the younger generation will build. I shall continue to hold my independent views and be loyal to my own friends for whom, and with whom, I have worked so long. But I can hardly find words sufficient to express my appreciation of the warmth of the welcome from my fellow townsmen.

After the meeting he was surrounded by numerous friends shaking his hand and congratulating him. He interested and amused them by showing them the white gloves which he had worn at his investiture by letting them into the secret that they were the gloves he had worn at his wedding in June 1872.[1] Arriving at last at his home he found scores of congratulatory letters and telegrams awaiting him from all parts of the country. The June meeting of the Fakenham Parish Council minuted its congratulation to George in the words of its chairman, 'We all know how he has worked for the benefit of mankind and has set an example for others to follow, and we all trust that he will be spared many years to enjoy it.'

The Primitive Methodist Church, to which he had given so many years of active service, paid tribute to his life's work and congratulated him on the honour bestowed upon him in an article in its official magazine, *The Aldersgate Magazine*. His own local church, the Buckenham Memorial Church, Fakenham, held a special civic service on the Sunday morning following his receipt of the honour. To this special service local councillors, local dignitaries and trade union leaders were invited. In the days that followed when he was touring the villages addressing various meetings and gatherings on behalf of the union, his church or the labour party, he found it difficult to accept being called 'Sir'. Often he would say to his union members, 'Now boys, you need not call me 'Sir', I am still your 'George' and I want you to call me that.' He always emphatically insisted upon this form of address from his friends and colleagues. But it was another story when confronted by those who had often been snobbish in their attitude to him and who appeared to look down upon the agricultural worker. These he insisted should address him correctly as 'Sir'. Once when he was in Norwich attending a county council meeting he met a certain gentleman from whom he had often, especially during his early years on the county council experienced an attitude of sarcasm and class consciousness. The gentleman had often derided George and his colleagues. On this particular occasion he greeted him as 'George'. To this George quickly and quietly replied, 'Sir George to you Sir.' The gentleman coloured and immediately apologised for his forgetfulness, much to the amusement of George's colleagues who were present. An elderly farm worker of Coltishall, who had been a loyal member of the union since the beginning, after George's elevation to the knighthood, always greeted him at union demonstrations at Coltishall, as 'Saint George'. This summed up the extent to which he had become revered by the majority of the agricultural workers in Norfolk. They were not slow in recognising the great and valuable work he had done and was still endeavouring to do on their behalf.

Notes

1. The gloves are still in good condition and in the possession of the author. They were worn by the author's youngest daughter at her wedding in August 1970.

Chapter 13

'Troubled Waters'

Among those named in the King's birthday honour's list at the same time as George was his old friend, Noel Buxton. He received a peerage and thus became Lord Noel-Buxton. This necessitated a by-election in North Norfolk and Lady Noel-Buxton was nominated as candidate. This was rather a strange turn of events, because before she had married Noel Buxton she had been a Conservative and had in fact canvassed against him. It was a point her Conservative opponents made much play upon in the by-election she was now fighting for Labour. At one of her meetings a leading Tory asked her if it were true that she had once been a Conservative, to which she replied 'Yes'. Then he asked, 'And then a Liberal and now a Socialist?' She replied, 'Yes, step by step I have advanced until I have reached the best party of all.' This silenced her questioner.

George very eagerly entered the election fight on her behalf, speaking and taking the chair at numerous meetings every evening throughout the constituency. His front room became the Fakenham Labour committee room, and he put up the visiting national agents and some of the speakers at his home. The election aroused quite a bit of excitement in the constituency. Prominent national speakers of both parties came in support of their respective candidates. It was about this time that a few leading Norfolk Farmers' Union men allied themselves to the Agricultural Party sponsored by Lord Beaverbrook and Lord Rothermere, under the name of 'Empire Crusaders.' Their aim was said to be to 'embrace the great army of small-holders and agricultural workers thrown out of employment.' Some time prior to the election they had approached George with the vain hope that he might ally himself with them. But finding it impossible to persuade him to forsake his friends at the NUAW, he was confronted with abuse. They labelled him as a paid socialist agitator. This did not worry him. Rather did it prove to him that his suspicions were true concerning the claims of the so called 'Empire Crusaders,' that it was to further the interests of the employing community and Tory party. However, on this occasion their efforts to defeat Lady Noel-Buxton proved fruitless. She was elected by a small majority.

It was not surprising that George's unceasing efforts and activity during this by-election should result in severely straining his heart and general physical condition. Despite the continued warnings to go slow by his doctor, his concern over the general agricultural scene would not allow him to rest with an easy mind. With the progress of the sugar beet industry some of the land workers found their jobs had become seasonal. Unemployment among them was on the increase, and there was not yet any unemployment benefit for farm workers. Many were impelled to seek poor law relief. To obtain this it was necessary for them to obtain the signatures of six employers testifying that they had no work to offer them. This meant they had often to travel many miles from village to village. Not only were the workers suffering poverty, but as always there was the threat of eviction from the tied cottage in which most of them lived. They naturally questioned why the Labour government, whom they had helped by their votes to put into office, did not do more to ease the situation for them. Particularly they felt sore that the tied cottage had not been abolished, and that they were still denied unemployment insurance benefit.

The National Union of Agricultural Workers and the Transport and General Workers Union sent a deputation to the national executive of the Labour party in the House of Commons to bring to the party's attention the worsening conditions of the agricultural worker. George was a member of this deputation. They did not mince matters. They urged swift government action. Unfortunately this meeting did not bring forth the required results. Nevertheless the loyalty of the majority of George's colleagues within the union ranks, particularly in Norfolk, to the Labour cause remained steadfast. He was very much aware of what this loyalty was costing many of them - not only materially, but mentally and physically. Because of this awareness he continued to visit as many of them in their homes and at their branch meetings giving them advice and always trying to keep their spirits up.

One of these loyal workers was a young man named Harry Flegg of Walsingham. He, with his father, had given most courageous and conscientious service to the union in the Walsingham area. Harry's father had recently been presented with a gold medal by George on behalf of the union in appreciation of the twenty-three years' service as branch secretary. Harry's health had become seriously affected, probably because of his strenuous outdoor activity for the cause he held so dear. He became very ill. On 13 March 1931, only a few days after George had visited him, Harry died. It came as a shock to George, although not entirely unexpected. He wrote a glowing tribute to Harry's life which was published in the local press.

Whilst he devoted a great deal of time to political and union affairs, George did not neglect his other public work. He continued to be very much involved in local affairs of his town and district. Progress was still very slow in the countryside. His own home town of Fakenham lacked many of the amenities that larger towns and urban areas possessed. There were slums and bad sanitary conditions both in the town and district and no piped water supply. In Fakenham at this time water was drawn from wells and pumps. The supply for council houses was drawn from a well by means of a windmill pump and piped to the houses. On one occasion in January 1930 the tenants of the adjoining parish of Hempton were without water for ten days because of a breakdown of the pump. Water had been ordered to be taken to them in a water-cart to meet the emergency, but somehow this was not done. At the rural district council meeting, George queried why proper action had not been taken. He moved a resolution deploring the situation. His action helped to hasten relief to the tenants.

With the lack of such necessary facilities in the town and district causing situations like that, it is surprising that the ratepayers generally seemed very reluctant to follow George and other progressive-minded people in demanding them. In fact in March 1931, a Fakenham parochial electors meeting turned down by a majority of ninety-six a water supply scheme for that parish. Fifty-three supported the demand for the implementation of a water scheme and 149 opposed it.

On 28 June of that year the union held a great demonstration at Fakenham. The principal speakers with the Rt Hon. F.O. Roberts, Minister of Pensions, and Mr F.A. Broad, MP. Mr George Hewitt presided and George took an active part in it. The demonstration was led by a silver band. They marched about a mile from the market place to Hempton Green where speeches were made from a wagon. A collection was taken to defray expenses. The speakers made glowing references to the work George had done for the land worker. They urged the younger generation to follow his example of courage and loyalty. After the demonstration in the afternoon they adjourned for tea. The visiting speaker and union officials had their tea with George at his home. For those people staying for the evening demonstration, he had arranged for a local caterer to provide tea on a meadow adjoining the caterer's premises. It was an occasion George always looked forward to very much because it gave him an opportunity to meet old friends and colleagues, discuss problems affecting the agricultural industry and talk over their varied experiences.

August that year saw a serious national financial crisis which led to the prime minister, Ramsay Macdonald, leaving his Labour colleagues to form a National Government (a coalition of some Labour cabinet ministers with the Tories). George had always been a great admirer of Ramsay Macdonald. But this action by the Labour premier left him deeply shocked and dismayed. He was convinced it was a betrayal of the whole working class movement. He firmly believed it could only result in 'putting the clock back' and undoing much of his and other Labour pioneer's work. He had had for some years a large framed photography of Ramsay Macdonald standing in a prominent

7. Sir George Edwards, president of the South Norfolk Labour Party with Sir Thomas Cook, Conservative MP for North Norfolk, and his daughter in 1931.

position in his home which he used to point out proudly to his friends as the picture of a great leader and great personality. However, following Ramsay's action he removed it and put it in a cupboard.

George realised the effect that Ramsay Macdonald's action would have upon those Labour MP's who had refused to follow his lead, as did those in Norfolk. He was determined to give them all the support he could in the general election which was soon to follow. The declaration of the poll showed that Labour had been severely defeated throughout the country. Once more abuse was heaped upon George and his colleagues. Union jacks were waved in their faces as they were greeted by their opponents singing the National Anthem and then jeering and booing them.

The election result combined with the general attitude of so many of those for whom George and his colleagues had devoted their life's efforts, left him most depressed. Some of his colleagues were so embittered that they declared that never again would they lift a hand to help the workers. They said 'let them stew in their own juice this time.' But George's sorrow and depression did not make him as embittered as that.

> I will not refuse to help them, although they sneered at me ... they are only carried away by misrepresentation. They will need all the help and pity they can get before long, unless I am much mistaken. We shall see when this new National Government really gets to work on them.

With this end in view he kept up his efforts on their behalf on both the rural district and county council. He continued to help his union to maintain the strength and loyalty of its members, although there was much apathy within its ranks. Branch meetings were poorly attended. In an endeavour to awaken new interest and to stimulate action to overcome the effects of government legislation and to prepare to ensure its defeat at the next general election, George formed a small band of speakers in his home district. Amongst these were Friday Layton and George Howes of Sculthorpe. They jokingly called themselves the 'Shoe-string Gang.' Every evening they would tour the villages of the district, urging the men to stand fast and keep within the ranks of the union.

In addition to these evening meetings, there were the Sunday demonstrations arranged by the union. A few days before he was due to speak at one of these at Holt, he received an anonymous letter in which the writer threatened that if George attended this demonstration his life would be in danger. He did not take it very seriously or worry unduly about it. But his friends persuaded him to hand the letter over to the police who deemed it sufficiently serious to insist that they should give him protection. He had told them that he would most certainly not stop away from the Holt demonstration and thus had the unusual experience of being escorted to and from his home by a police motor cyclist riding in front of his car and one behind. Arriving at Holt and the place of the demonstration he found a strong police guard awaiting him. They remained close to him throughout the afternoon meeting. However, no untoward event, not even any heckling occurred. The incident was soon forgotten in the days that followed.

The implementation of the means test showed George that his forecast of what the result of the National Government's measures upon the worker would be had come true. He was inundated with letters from those seeking his help and advice. Hardly an evening passed without numerous people calling upon him begging him to do what he could to assist them. Among them he recognised some of those who had sneeringly jeered at him, and some who had joined his opponents in denouncing him during the general election campaign. Whilst he quietly reminded them of their attitude on that occasion, he never once refused to listen to their tales of woe or to help them if he possibly could.

These activities of his left him very little free time during the week or on Sundays. For Sunday was never really a day of rest for him. Although he took part in some Sunday union demonstrations, he never neglected his preaching or attending his home church. He also continued to help churches and circuits both in Norfolk and further afield. He still received requests for him to give his life story at various town and village chapels. He had by this time given it at almost 500 places. His yearly invitation to conduct special services at Elm, near Wisbech, soon came round again. This meant a week-end away from home. He would stay with an old friend, Mr Burman, who had been one of the first members of his union in that district. Mr Burman had, however, had the good fortune to get on in business as a fruit grower and market gardener. He had by this time acquired much land and was one of the biggest fruit growers in that district. With his progress in business he had changed politically and now professed to being a Tory. But he disagreed at that time with the Tory party's policy of protection and tariffs, believing that it would ultimately lead to war.

George found great enjoyment during these week-ends with his old friend. They had many a friendly argument on the political issues of the day.

Mrs Burman would take her husband into Wisbech in his car on the Saturday morning to buy a daily paper. He would get the *Daily Mail* for himself and the *Daily Herald* for George. Handing George his paper he would say to him, 'Here's your red rag, George!' On his last visit to Elm, George was amazed to see on entering his friend's house the *Daily Herald* upon the armchair. With a smile George said, 'Not the red rag in this house, surely?' 'Yes' was the reply, 'I'm converted at last, thanks partly to your powers of persuasion.' George was indeed surprised and overjoyed to hear this, but with mock sadness said, 'That's a pity, now we shan't have anything to argue about this time.' 'Oh yes we will,' Mr Burman replied. 'What about Methodist Union? I hear you're a staunch supporter of it. Well I don't believe in it. I'm dead against it. I cannot see any good coming out of it.' So it was that, with no political argument to engage in, these two very good friends had an enjoyable week-end arguing the pros and cons of Methodist Union. Each vehemently defending his own view and trying to convert the other unsuccessfully to it.

As was to be expected the very full and active life George returned to, in complete disregard of his doctor's warning, began to affect his health once more. He would often, to those closest to him, appear to be quite his old self, cheerful and 'fit as a fiddle' when suddenly he would be attacked by a feeling of giddiness. His head jerked backwards and he would have fallen to the ground had not Miss Myers or someone else been close beside him and had hold of his arm to steady him. Prior to these attacks his deafness, now permanent, would increase to render him stone deaf. It became a warning sign for him to go steady. But he did not always heed the warning.

At the beginning of 1932, whilst attending a district council meeting, one of these attacks came on and he had to be brought home. The doctor insisted that he should stay in bed for a few days. It was during this period that a rumour reached a relative and some friends living at Bodham, near Holt, that he had died. A letter was received expressing sorrow and concern and inquiring when the funeral would be. The embarrassment of those sending the inquiry can well be imagined when the truth became known to them. However, George was always able to see the humorous side of things and was not in the least offended. He quickly made light of it and put his relative and friends at ease.

From this illness he made a remarkably speedy recovery. Soon he was out and about again and even well enough to travel to London to attend his union's biennial conference on 6 May 1932. He took part in a very lively and forceful debate upon a resolution supporting the abolition of the tithe in opposition to the view held by his friend the union's president, Edwin Gooch. George said that he had always been in favour of disestablishment and disendowment. He held the view that the time had long gone by when any individual man or woman should be compelled by law to contribute to any form of religion that he or she felt they had no use for.

> But, this was quite a different problem. This resolution did nothing of that kind. All it does is to take up the agitation against the Act of 1925. A number of those (farmers) who were now leading the movement bought their land knowing full well the liabilities they had to meet in reference to it. Who were the leaders of the movement? Why, they are the very men who last October had told the people to elect the present ramshackle, dishonest and wicked government. Now the election was over they came along and wanted their assistance. I want to say that no industry in this country had had so much done for it as agriculture, but like Oliver Twist, every time these people wanted something more. I am old enough to remember the agitation seventy years ago when there was compulsory church rate; and that was repealed. But did the leaders of that day come to the farm worker and say, 'We have got relief from our taxes, we will give you another bob?' No, directly it was passed they reduced wages from ten shillings to nine shillings a week. Then another agitation took place in regard to ground game, and they got that also. Agriculture at that time was prospering. Did they come and say 'You can have a rabbit or a hare?' No. Directly there were prosecutions and they put the screw on the agricultural worker. They should not trouble themselves about the burden that was lying on the land. It was not their question; it was the farmers' and the landlord's question.

Mr Gooch replied and put the other viewpoint:

> In supporting this agitation for the removal of at least a part of the burden of the tithe, I have not the slightest idea of supporting the farmers as individuals. Why on earth should the burden of supporting the National Church be placed upon one industry in the land? I cannot understand it. There is a lot of money that was collected in the form of tithes that did not even go to the Church.

Mr Gooch believed it went to the support of the universities of Oxford and Cambridge. They were surely not going to tell him it was a right principle that the children of the high and mighty in the land should be enjoying an education that their children were denied, partly at their expense. He then continued,

When I made my first speech in support of this idea of lifting the burden of tithes from the land I told the meeting of farmers quite plainly where I stood. I told them it was a unique experience for me to be speaking at a meeting of farmers, and I also told them quite plainly that the first word I heard to the detriment of the labourers in regard to wages and hours, on that day I would walk out of the door and never return.

He said they had not thought about reducing wages and increasing hours. All they were concerned about was to get a Tithe Remission Bill passed that would have the effect of repealing what he considered unjust in the Tithe Act of 1925. In conclusion, Mr Gooch said, 'I am solely concerned for this principle and because I believe that the principle of tithes was vicious I support the Tithe Remission Bill. If I thought the tithe agitation was aiming a blow at the church I would not support it.'[1] The resolution when put to the conference was carried.

Although George's physical strength had become much weaker as his years had advanced, the active part he took in this biennial conference showed that his intellect and debating powers remained as strong as ever, as did his radical ideas. But it had become notable of late that he had occasionally become a little absent-minded. This caused him some embarrassment, but it was not of a serious nature and more often than not caused himself as well as those closest to him some amusing moments. Such was the case when one day he could not find his clean vest, when dressing. He looked everywhere for it without success. A little later he discovered he was wearing two, having put a clean one over the one he wished to change.

Another thing which gave him some concern was that he was continually having strange dreams and nightmares. His mind appeared as alert during his sleep as during the day. In these days he would go back to the days of his early youth, previous to his conversion to christianity. He would find himself being confronted by his bullying employer. In the midst of this he would suddenly burst forth into song, singing at the top of his voice the old ranter gospel tunes, one of which was 'Hark the Gospel news is sounding,' but the words were not those of the hymn but 'Go you to buggery,' interspersed with other violent swear words aimed at his antagonistic employer. Upon one occasion, George, having had his session of singing and swearing at the farmer, suddenly climbed out of bed and ran to the bedroom door. He flung it open and proceeded to go out, but unfortunately there was a clothes trunk nearby over which he stumbled. Getting to his feet he shouted at the top of his voice, 'The bloody old farmer has thrown me over the hedge.' The noise he made woke the whole household who quickly came to his aid. Luckily he suffered no ill effect from his fall and was put safely back to bed where he slept soundly without any further disturbance until the morning.

When he awoke after these experiences he could remember nothing of them and suffered no ill effects. But he occasionally had a nightmare quite different from these other dreams. He would appear to wake suddenly in the middle of the night. He would get up and go to the window and pull the curtain aside. After being helped back to bed he would protest and say, 'My dear wife is outside and can't get in, I must go and let her in.' These nightmares left him restless until morning and appeared to react upon his health the following day. These nightly experiences, though most of them of the humorous type, worried him in case they should happen in the home of friend when taking religious services or being away from home for other commitments. This happened once, and on that occasion he had his adopted son with him and he was awakened before he could disturb anyone else. Nevertheless he decided to seek his doctor's advice. The doctor told him that it was the result of a very active life and the great suffering he had experienced in his early years reacting upon his subconscious mind. The doctor added, 'I could stop them, but it would stop you too.'

On 12 June 1932, George led a procession to the New Walsingham churchyard following a union demonstration in the market place. There he unveiled a memorial to his late friend, Harry Flegg, who had been a loyal and faithful member of the union and was one of those involved in the 1923 Norfolk strike. The inscription on the memorial read:

> Erected by members of the National Union of Agricultural Workers
> In Memory of Arthur Henry Flegg,
> Died March 15th, 1931, aged 39 years.
> 'He who in Fealty to the Truth,
> And counting all the cost,
> Does consecrate his generous Youth,
> He joins the Noble Host.'

Two weeks later George took part in another great demonstration. It was the annual Norfolk county demonstration of his union at Hempton Green, Fakenham. The principal speakers were the Rt Hon. George Lansbury, MP, then leader of the parliamentary Labour Party, and Mr Ben Tillet, the docker's leader of the 'Docker's Tanner' fame. George Lansbury came to Fakenham from Norwich, but Ben Tillet stayed with George, who was greatly amused by Ben's habit of taking out his false teeth before each meal, putting them in his serviette, salting them and proceeding to eat without them. George very much enjoyed exchanging experiences with Ben. Ben was renowned for his blunt and crude form of speech and his typical dockers' expressions were an embarrassment to many, but George found him a sincere and good-natured personality and a likeable character.

A month later, 29 July, George received the sad news of the passing of his friend W.B. Taylor at the early age of fifty-seven. 'WB' had been in indifferent health for some time but the end was rather sudden. He had played a very prominent and useful part in the work of the Labour movement and the agricultural workers' union with George in Norfolk, although he was himself a farmer. Like George, he was a county alderman and he had represented South-West Norfolk in parliament. He was one of the defeated candidates at the previous general election. 'WB' had refused to follow the lead of Ramsay MacDonald into the Tory camp. His death came as a great blow to George who held him in high esteem as a very dear and close friend. When he received the news he sat down in his chair, and wept. A memorial service was held for 'WB' on 25 September at the Swaffham Cinema. It was conducted by the Revd Fred J. Hopkins. The hymns 'Fight the good fight' and 'O God of Bethel by whose hand' were followed by addresses given by George, Alderman Witard, JP, of Norwich and Mr E.G. Gooch. During the course of his address George said:

> Brother Taylor was sound in judgement and all his actions were guided by common-sense. He was moderate in his outlook on the great political and social problems of the day, especially agriculture, and whilst a loyal and strong supporter of the labourers and their union, he always endeavoured to do his best to keep peace between employer and employed. So great was his conciliatory spirit that some of his colleagues sometimes were afraid he would go a little too far in that direction, but I never thought so. I, with him, held the conviction that you cannot go too far in that direction unless you jeopardise the interests of the workers, which he never did. His outlook and mine on these great problems were so much in common that what little difference there was that existed was very soon adjusted. I always found him a most loyal colleague, kindly of heart and the closest friendship existed between us, and I feel in his passing away that I have lost a dear and personal friend.

The addresses were followed by the hymn 'Lord of the living harvest,' and the benediction. Before the service George also opened a Memorial Hall in

Swaffham to the memory of W.B. Taylor. This has since been closed and the memory of 'WB' with that of his successor as Labour member for South-West Norfolk, Sidney Dye, is maintained in a new Memorial Hall called the Sidney Dye Memorial Hall at Swaffham.

Notes

1.   From Conference report in *The Landworkers*, July 1932.

Chapter 14

'George, Fare Thee Well'

The Christmas of 1932 George spent quietly at home. He reflected upon the events of the past two years. Years in which the workers had experienced unemployment and the means test. He and his colleagues had had a very strenuous fight upon the wages committee to ensure the defeat of the bitter attack upon the agricultural workers' wages. The years had seen the loss of his close friends within the Labour and trade union movement. Naturally these events left him feeling rather depressed. He was now eighty-two years old. He wondered if his efforts had really made any worthwhile impact upon his fellows or their problems. How much longer would he be spared to continue his efforts? So depressed did he feel that he remarked, with tears in his eyes, 'Well, I reckon I too shall be under the sod next Christmas.'

His mood of depression, together with the fact that his health was not too good either at that time, gave some cause for concern. His head had been troubling him again, so that he was compelled to spend a few days in bed. But, he was well enough to be able to get up to join in the Christmas festivities, and insisted upon making his customary Christmas Eve treacle toffee. Early in 1933, his old buoyant spirit returned. Despite the fact that his weakened heart made him ease up considerably on his public activity, his general health seemed greatly improved. He was determined not to give up completely and insisted upon attending as many union meetings as he could. His preaching appointments of course had to be reduced, but he would not hear of giving up preaching altogether, or neglect any of his religious responsibilities any more than he could possibly help.

It was always difficult to ensure that he did not over-exert himself in these activities. Miss Myers and his friends watched over him most carefully. They were constantly by his side. Occasionally they managed to persuade him not to address a meeting. His colleagues who organised the meetings assured him that his presence greatly helped and encouraged both themselves and the workers. At other times he was only allowed to speak for a few moments or to preside. The previous September, a church parade had been inaugurated at Carbrooke, near Watton, in connection with the union. It was sponsored through the invitation of the then vicar and his wife, the Revd and Mrs G.B. Chambers. For 1933 it was held on 16 June in the church and upon the vicarage lawn. George loved this service. He would have been bitterly disappointed had he been prevented from attending. His closest friends were a little apprehensive in case it overtaxed his strength, particularly when he took a prominent part in it as on this occasion. At his request he opened the service and read the lessons. The service began with a hymn, followed by the lesson. A musical selection was given by a silver band and followed by the second lesson. After reading the lessons George retired to a seat in the vicarage, where he was given a cup of tea and was able to watch the service proceeding upon the lawn. George had hoped this service would become an annual event, and this was agreed. He said he wished there were more services like it, adding, 'without the Spirit of Christ and a religious foundation our work, and the whole Labour movement will be in vain.'

In previous chapters we saw how among George's many local activities had been his support, both on and off the Fakenham parish council, for the provision of a playing field. Victory came to those who had continued to work for this amenity in September 1933 when a Fakenham parochial meeting voted in favour of Fakenham Parish Council buying land in Queen's Road near the school by a majority of 211 to 52. In early November the parish council was told that the contract had been signed and by December it was finalised. That this was accomplished during George's last days brought him much comfort and joy.

The continuing hardships resulting from the means test determined him to continue his efforts on the Walsingham Rural District Council to alleviate these hardships within his home district. He missed few meetings of this body or the board of guardians. Although he was not feeling too well on 22 November, when a board of guardians meeting was due to be held, and despite efforts to persuade him not to go, he went to the meeting at Thursford workhouse. There he entered enthusiastically into the business, particularly that of a case concerning a land worker and his wife who were threatened with eviction. His last recorded words upon this council were in connection with this case. 'I want,' he said, 'to know whether anything can be done for these unfortunate people. The clerk will tell us that this council has no legal obligation, but I say that at least we have a moral obligation to see that these people have a house to live in. This ought to be our first consideration.'

He was filled with emotion as he spoke. It cost him no little effort and he collapsed, suffering from a heart attack. He was helped from the meeting and taken home. During the night he had another attack and the doctor had to be hurriedly called. By next morning he showed signs of improvement and took his food fairly normally. He was confined to bed completely for a few days and then allowed up for a few hours at a time. The Wednesday following George had another mild attack during the day, but it was not necessary to call the doctor as an inhalant he had prescribed resulted in a quick recovery, However, during the early hours of Thursday morning another more severe attack came on and the doctor had to be sent for. George himself felt that the end was near and called Miss Myers and his adopted son to his side. They watched by him for an hour or two when sleep seemed to improve his condition. The improvement continued throughout the day and for the next few days. But on the Tuesday of the following week he appeared not so well again.

North Norfolk Constituency Labour Party had been holding meetings and social evenings in the district. One had been arranged at Fakenham for this particular Tuesday evening. George had heard reports that these had not been very successful, and he was disappointed at not being able to attend any of them, especially the Fakenham one. It caused him to be a little despondent. Lady Noel-Buxton attended the Fakenham social evening after which she called to hear how he was progressing and brought him a hand portrait of Joseph Arch. As he was not so well again she refused to disturb him. He did not know until much later that she had been.

Another attack that night led to the doctor being called. His condition remained indifferent during the early hours of the following day 6 December. By lunch time he was able to sit up for a few minutes in his armchair. He said he was feeling a lot better, and looked it. He was a great deal more cheerful than he had been of late. He said he was sure he would be fit enough to get up and dress in a few days, adding, 'There's no need to worry about me now, I'm better.' He had his tea about five o'clock and remarked, 'It's the best meal I've had for days.' He appeared to get catarrh in his throat which made him cough severely. There followed a severe heart attack which the inhalant failed to overcome. He reeled back into Miss Myer's arms and quietly passed away before the doctor arrived. The doctor said had he been present when the attack came on he could have done nothing to save him. The heart was really worn out due to the continuation of his strenuous activity in public work at a time when many others would have given up. Had he not done so, he would probably have lived for many more years.

The news of his death was soon flashed throughout the country. The Norfolk newspapers announced it the next day in large bold headlines. Telegrams and letters of condolence were received from all parts from people of various shades of religious and political thought. Many agricultural workers and his union colleagues could hardly believe the news to be true. Although George's age and weakened health had long caused them to recognise the end of this great life could not be too far distant, now it had come they were filled with deep shock and sorrow, a gloom seemed to have settled upon them.

George was carried to his last resting place on the following Monday, 11 December 1933. The funeral service was held in the Buckenham Memorial Methodist Church, Fakenham. It was filled to overflowing, many being unable to get in. The Revd F.A. Ingham, superintendent minister of the Fakenham and Wells Circuit, conducted the service. He paid tribute to a man 'Fair in his judgement, deliberate in speech, courteous in conversation, fearless in denunciation of any form of oppression or wrong. He kept troth.' George's favourite hymns, 'Lead Kindly Light,' and 'Fight the Good Fight'

8. Sir George's funeral cortege leaves Fakenham Methodist Church, December 1933.

were sung. On the way to the Fakenham Cemetery the cortege passed through the town where it seemed people of all walks of life lined the streets to pay their last respects to a great man. All places of business were shut as the procession passed by. Outside the Queen's Road school, near the cemetery, the children were lined up with their teachers to pay their last respects to one who had championed the cause of youth in the town, and served their interests upon the county education committee.

At the graveside were hundreds more people, representatives of all local public bodies, the National Union of Agricultural Workers, the National Farmers' Union, North Norfolk Labour, Conservative and Liberal Parties and all religious denominations of the town and district. Many wreaths covered the coffin and hearse. Many more were brought to place on the grave afterwards. Tears were seen in many an eye. George had always been fond of brass band music. He had long been an ardent supporter of various village bands and the Fakenham town band in particular. Each Christmas Eve, when the band toured the Fakenham streets playing carols, they always stopped outside his house and played his favourite hymn. On these occasions he would get up from his bed and stand by the window and acknowledge their kind thought. He had requested that they should play at his graveside.

One other request that George had made was also fulfilled. It was that his friend of many years, Walter Smith, should make a parting address at the graveside. This was done in a most moving and statesmanlike way. Showing the deep emotion and sorrow he sincerely felt, Walter Smith said:

> Our old comrade has laid upon me the task of saying a few words at this our final leave-taking. I first met him forty years ago, and it is twenty-five years since we began a very close association. This enables me to say that in his passing Norfolk has lost one of its greatest sons ... He was great in the sacrifice and effort made on behalf of his own people. He never spoke ill of anyone. Even those who had treated him harshly he spoke of it in terms of sorrow more than anger ... In his humble, simple way he seemed to believe and feel they would meet their reward and that it was not for him to pass judgement upon them ... Though he was gentle with those who had injured him personally, he display indignation and passion for the wrongs that his fellows suffered. He spoke with a force and eloquence never excelled on the village green and seldom on the platform. He believed he was engaged in a deeply religious work and he threw his whole heart and soul into it. He had great courage. He feared no man ... Therefore in taking leave of him today surely we can say of him, if of any human being, 'Well done, thou good and faithful servant. Enter thou into the joy of thy Lord'. George, fare thee well. We shall see that your memory is ever green. We will try to carry on to a completed finish the work to which you so well contributed and gave the whole of your devoted life.

The press next day gave much space to the account of George's life and report of his funeral with many pictures illustrating different spheres of his activities. The following Sunday a united church memorial service was held in the Buckenham Memorial Methodist Church at Fakenham. This was attended by members of parish and district councils, local trade union and Labour officials. It was conducted by the Revd Mr Ingham. Once more George's favourite hymns were sung.

Many times George had found that his efforts on behalf of the poor were derided. Often the accusation had been thrown at him, 'You wouldn't do it if you weren't paid for it.' But now he had gone the time to settle his estate had come. After the funeral and sundry expenses had been paid there was left a balance of ten pounds. His household effects were left to his adopted son (the author) to whom he had already passed on many of his books and documents relating to political, religious and local government work. The remainder of his books he bequeathed to his colleagues, Walter Smith and George Hewitt, with the request that they should ensure they were made available to those workers who were not able to purchase or obtain books for themselves.

The trade union and Labour movement organised a memorial service on 7 January 1934 in the Fakenham Central Cinema. Addresses were given by Mr E.G. Gooch (President of the NUAW), Mr William Holmes (General Secretary, NUAW), Ald. George Hewitt, Ald. H.E. Witard (member of Norwich City Council Labour group), Lord Noel-Buxton and the Revd G.B. Chambers (Vicar of Carbrooke). Music was provided by the Fakenham Town and Salvation Army bands. People from far and wide and of all walks of life were there.

Inquiries had begun through various organisations and spheres of public life in which George had been actively engaged and interested in as to the possibility of a permanent memorial being erected to him. Shortly after the memorial service the National Union of Agricultural Workers set up a fund for this purpose. It was finally decided that it should take the form of a stone of Cornish granite to symbolise his rock-like loyalty, steadfast courageous determination. It was to be seven feet high with a bust of his head and shoulders made of Italian marble. There was some delay in acquiring the marble due to the Abyssinian war. It was feared that it might not be possible to obtain it at all. However, it eventually arrived enabling the memorial to be erected. It bears the following inscription:

> Sacred to the undying memory of Sir George Edwards, KBE, JP,
> Born October 5th, 1850, Died December 6th, 1933
> This memorial is erected by the National Union of Agricultural Workers, which organisation he founded in 1906, and whose members greatly valued his wise counsel and his delightful companionship throughout the years. To the ideals of our Movement and the people of his choice he remained true to the end.
> Well done, thou good and faithful Servant'

(and on the back of the memorial)

> The agricultural worker who became successively Parish, District and County Councillor, County Alderman, Justice of the Peace for Norfolk, Chairman of the Parish Council for this Town, Member of Parliament in two Parliaments, Knight of the British Empire, etc, Honoured by King and Country he ever remained humble, striving to improve the social conditions of the people, and giving services to the poor. He lived to see much of the fruit of his labours, and the memory of his life of service will ever remain as an inspiration to those who carry on his work.
> 'Life's race well run. Life's work well done.'

The memorial was unveiled on Sunday 13 October 1935, by Edwin Gooch. The day was cold, but bright. About a thousand people attended the ceremony: the deep silences during the prayers, the singing of the hymns and the reading of the scriptures made it a very moving and impressive service.

Following the unveiling ceremony, addresses were given by Mr Tom Smith, MP who represented the Parliamentary Labour party. He briefly recalled George's work in Parliament; Mr A. Findlay, Chairman of the TUC, who recalled the wider influence that had been caused to be made in the whole trade union movement for the agricultural workers; Mr W. Holmes, President of the National Union of Agricultural Workers, who gave a brief resume of George's early struggles and triumphs in face of great odds. Also present was Mr Walter Smith and representatives of local and constituency Labour parties, parish, district and county councils. The family was represented by George's adopted son (the author) and Miss Myers (the late Mrs W. Dalton). At the close of the service the town band played, 'Lead Kindly Light'.

A service of remembrance at the graveside started to be held each year on May Day when a wreath on behalf of the union was placed on the grave. On May Day 1949, the then prime minister, Clement Attlee, accompanied by Mrs Attlee, attended and placed a wreath. A very large gathering was

9. The Prime Minister, Clement Atlee, speaking at the grave of Sir George Edwards in Fakenham Cemetery, May Day, 1949.

present. In recent years it has been mostly a small group of friends, relatives and trade unionists who have gathered. Arthur Amis, the stalwart Methodist preacher and trade unionist of Trunch, who was involved in the 1923 strike, has taken part on each occasion. Periodically, organised parties and individuals have visited the grave to pay their silent tribute. The official union May Day ceremony ceased with the amalgamation of the National Union of Agricultural & Allied Workers with the Transport & General Workers Union.

In July 1983 the Gressenhall and Rural Life Museum commemorated the fiftieth anniversary of George's death by an exhibition of photographs, banners and items about his life, work and conditions of his early days. The Masque Theatre of Fakenham performed a musical play in the museum chapel entitled 'With Orphan Tears' based on a family and early union days of George's organising work. Many of the items exhibited then in the museum are today still on display.

On 9 June 1985, a commemoration service was held comprising a wreath-laying ceremony at Fakenham cemetery followed by a service in Marsham (George's birthplace) Methodist Chapel. This was organised by the methodist church through the Revd William Gowland (Principal of Luton Industrial College and a past president of the methodist conference), and the Marsham methodists. He was assisted both at Fakenham and Marsham services by the chairman of East Anglia district methodists, the Revd Richard Jones. At the graveside prayers were led by the superintendent of the Fakenham and Wells methodist circuit (Revd Arthur Kirkman) and a short tribute was given by Arthur Amis. Wreaths were laid by Revd Gowland on behalf of the methodist church, George Barnard on behalf of the union and Adrian Cunningham on behalf of the North Norfolk Constituency Labour Party. Among about 100 people present were Jack Boddy, representing the Agricultural & Allied Workers' Trade Group, the Rector of Fakenham and George's family.

At Marsham the service was led by Revd Gowland and Revd Jones. Greetings were given by Jack Boddy, George Barnard, Stephen Peart and the author, Noel Edwards. The principal speaker was Lord Murray of Epsom (Len Murray, past TUC General Secretary). About 400-500 people were present, the little chapel was packed full and others listened at the school field through a public address system. Through these and others to come we can ensure that George's sacrificial efforts will never be forgotten because:

> These things shall be a loftier race,
> Than e'er the world hath known shall rise,
> With flames of freedom in their souls,
> And light of knowledge in their eyes.

INDEX

155